DIESEL POWER
IN THE
NORTH
EASTERN
REGION

BRIAN J. DICKSON

The
History
Press

Front cover: **Wednesday 23 May 1962**. In spotless condition, D9007 *Pinza* is seen at the head of the Down 'Heart of Midlothian' near Berwick-upon-Tweed. Entering service during June 1961 she was named after the 1953 Derby winner and was allocated to Finsbury Park shed in London. She would be withdrawn from service during December 1981. *(Michael Mensing)*

Back cover: **Monday 20 April 1964**. This three-car Metro-Cammell Class 101 DMU has worked into Durham station early in the morning from Bishop Auckland and is parked in the Up bay platform awaiting its return duty later that day. *(J.M. Boyes/ARPT)*

First published 2013

The History Press
The Mill, Brimscombe Port
Stroud, Gloucestershire, GL5 2QG
www.thehistorypress.co.uk

© Brian J. Dickson, 2013

The right of Brian J. Dickson to be identified as the Author
of this work has been asserted in accordance with the
Copyrights, Designs and Patents Act 1988.

British Library Cataloguing in Publication Data.
A catalogue record for this book is available from the British Library.

ISBN 978 0 7524 9313 8

Typesetting and origination by The History Press
Printed in Great Britain
Manufacturing managed by Jellyfish Solutions Ltd

INTRODUCTION

With the nationalisation of the railways in January 1948, the rail network in the north-east of England had been placed within the North Eastern Region of British Railways, and given a distinctive orange 'corporate colour'. In late 1966 it was announced that from January 1967 the North Eastern Region would lose its autonomy and be merged with the Eastern Region, the headquarters of the new enlarged region to be in York. This book therefore shows diesel traction at work within the North Eastern Region up to its demise in December 1966 and afterwards as part of the enlarged Eastern Region.

In December 1954, when the British Transport Commission published its plan for the 'Modernisation and Re-equipment of British Railways', the number of main line diesels operating on British Railways was seven – the two LMS-designed Co-Cos (nos 10000/1), the Fell 2-D-2 locomotive (no. 10100), the three Southern Region 1Co-Co1s (nos 10201–3) and the LMS designed Bo-Bo (no. 10800) constructed by the North British Locomotive Co (NBL). The prototype Deltic did not arrive until the end of 1955.

Likewise, diesel shunting locomotives were relatively few; the LMS, GWR, SR and LNER had all invested in the 0–6–0 diesel 350hp-engined type prior to nationalisation and British Railways acquired approximately eighty of these from the four railways. It was 1953 before British Railways started to produce larger numbers of its own 0–6–0 diesel electric powered shunter closely modelled on the LMS type. The Modernisation Plan makes it clear that the elimination of shunting work by steam locomotives was to be achieved within fifteen years – by 1970! Thus it was that, by the late 1950s, various types of diesel shunters were working from North Eastern Region depots. These included the standard BR-constructed 350hp 0–6–0 diesel-electric (Class 08) and some Hunslet-built diesel mechanical 0–6–0 (Class 05) locomotives. As the plan envisaged, they were replacing steam shunting locomotives at such a rate that by 1960 a large amount of the shunting duties throughout the region were being carried out by diesels.

In locomotive terms the Modernisation Plan predicted the end of steam power by announcing that no new steam locomotives would be built after the end of the 1956 programme. Reasons cited were the difficulty of attracting labour for the tasks of cleaning, firing and servicing; the greater cleanliness of trains and stations; the demands for reduction in air pollution; the growing shortage of large coal suitable for steam locomotives and the need for better acceleration. Although the Plan also recognised the advantages of the steam locomotive, such as low first-build cost, simplicity, robustness and long life, it added that the end of the steam era was nigh.

Although electrification was the ultimate goal, diesel traction, particularly with electric transmission, was seen as the way forward, and an initial programme, the Pilot Scheme, was devised whereby 174 main line diesel locomotives would be purchased from various manufacturers – 160 with electric transmission and 14 with hydraulic transmission specifically for the Western Region. These were to be in three power groups:

Type A   600–1,000hp
Type B   1,000–1,250hp
Type C   2,000hp and over

These three groups would later become five:

Type 1   1,000hp or less
Type 2   1,000–1,500hp
Type 3   1,500–2,000hp
Type 4   2,000–3,000hp
Type 5   3,000hp and over

The initial orders fell into the groups shown in the table below.

Type	TPOS class	Builder	Engine Power	Wheel Arr	Transmission	Initial Order	Delivered	Number series
1	15	Clayton*	800hp	Bo-Bo	Electric	10	1957	D8200
1	16	NBL	800hp	Bo-Bo	Electric	10	1958	D8400
1	20	English Electric	1,000hp	Bo-Bo	Electric	20	1957	D8000
2	21	NBL	1,000hp	Bo-Bo	Electric	10	1958	D6100
2	22	NBL	1,000hp	B-B	Hydraulic	6	1958	D6300
2	23	English Electric	1,100hp	Bo-Bo	Electric	10	1959	D5900
2	24	BR Derby	1,160hp	Bo-Bo	Electric	20	1958	D5000
2	26	BRC&W	1,160hp	Bo-Bo	Electric	20	1958	D5300
2	28	Metro-Vick	1,200hp	Co-Bo	Electric	20	1958	D5700
2	30	Brush	1,250hp	A1A-A1A	Electric	20	1957	D5500
4	40	English Electric	2,000hp	1Co-Co1	Electric	10	1958	D200
4	41	NBL	2,000hp	A1A-A1A	Hydraulic	5	1957	D600
4	42	BR Swindon	2,000hp	B-B	Hydraulic	3	1958	D800
4	44	BR Derby	2,300hp	1Co-Co1	Electric	10	1959	D1

*Construction sub-contracted to Yorkshire Engine Co.

The initial intention was that, as the various types of Pilot Scheme locomotives were delivered, they would undergo intensive evaluation trials. But the policy soon changed to one whereby these locomotives were put into revenue-earning service as quickly as possible. To hasten the demise of steam many manufacturing orders were increased before completion of the initial orders. Hence such types as the NBL/MAN Type 2 (Class 21), although quickly recognised as having a troublesome engine, reached a final construction total of 58 locomotives.

The numbering for these new diesel locomotives had been fixed in 1957, prior to their introduction, with the use of a four-digit number and the 'D' prefix. Diesel shunters built prior to 1957 that bore five-figure numbers were allocated a new number with a 'D' prefix. In September 1968, with the end of standard-gauge steam on British Railways, the use of the 'D' prefix was discontinued. In practice, locomotives started to lose the 'D' prefix either when they went into the workshops for overhaul or when individual depots started to paint out the 'D'. Either way, a large number of locomotives kept the 'D' prefix for many years after the 1968 decision. A number of photographs in this book show locomotives between September 1968 and 1974 still proudly bearing the 'D'. In 1972 the present Total Operations Processing System (TOPS) was introduced, locomotives being allocated a two-digit class number followed

September 1955. This period saw the delivery of the second batch of 'Derby Lightweight' units to the North Eastern Region for service on Tyneside. This photograph shows an ex-works four-car unit approaching Darlington South signal-box en route to Newcastle. *(J. W. Armstrong/ARPT)*

by an individual serial number; thus, for example, English Electric Type 5 (Class 55) no. D9007 became 55 007.

By late 1952, the Light Weight Trains Committee of the Railway Executive had completed its report and in an effort to improve revenue from branch and cross-country services, announced a programme for the introduction of diesel multiple-units (DMUs). By April 1954 the first units had been delivered from Derby Works and in June of that year commenced operation on the local 'West Riding' services between Leeds and Bradford. These two-car units became known as 'Derby Lightweights'.

Early units from the second batch of these machines were allocated to operate in West Cumberland and later deliveries were by November 1955 seen operating on South Tyneside routes. Following the success of these early units the Railway Executive placed orders with the Metropolitan-Cammell Carriage and Wagon Co. (Metro-Cammell) for the construction of further examples of two-, three- and four-car units which were introduced during 1956, eventually becoming designated Class 101 in TOPS. Building continued until 1960 with many seeing service throughout the North Eastern Region. DMUs from other manufacturers were also to be seen operating in the region with Birmingham Railway Carriage & Wagon Co. (BRC&W) Class 104s and BR Derby-built Class 108s becoming more common during the late 1950s and early 1960s. Another of the early successes was the introduction in July 1960 of powerful Swindon-built six-car Class 124 units to the 'Trans-Pennine' service running between Hull and Liverpool; taking just under three hours to complete the journey the sets included a buffet car which proved very popular with passengers.

In January 1962 the North Eastern Region introduced BRC&W Class 110 units to the 'Calder Valley' route between Leeds and Manchester. Specifically designed to operate over this difficult cross-Pennine line via Todmorden, they proved successful and the units continued in operation until the early 1990s.

While the introduction of DMUs was proceeding, the first batches of main line diesel locomotives were being delivered from the builders. In 1957, the first examples of the English Electric Type 1 (Class 20) were being delivered, with further batches rapidly following as BR quickly increased the order. These were primarily allocated to the London Midland Region with a few early examples going to Scottish Region depots in the north of that country. The same year also saw the first of the Brush-built Type 2 (Class 30) locomotives coming into service with the largest number being allocated to the Eastern Region. These Class 30 locomotives were originally constructed with a Mirrlees engine that proved to be unreliable in service. The answer to the problem was to re-engine the whole class with a more reliable English Electric engine. The work took place between January 1965 and the summer of 1969, the re-engined locomotives being designated Class 31.

By the middle of 1958 Derby Works had started to deliver the initial batch of its Pilot Scheme Type 2 (Class 24) locomotives. Powered by Sulzer engines, they very quickly became one of the most widely allocated and successful Pilot Scheme Type 2 designs. Further batches were constructed at Derby, Crewe and Darlington works and later examples, powered by a more powerful engine and with some exterior design modifications, became Class 25 in TOPS. Eighteen of the early examples of Class 24 were allocated to Gateshead and Thornaby depots and the first twenty-five examples of Class 25 were also allocated to these depots. October 1959 saw the arrival at Gateshead depot of the first of an allocation of eleven examples of the very successful English Electric Type 4 (Class 40) for express passenger duties on the East Coast Main Line and by 1962 both Gateshead and York depots each had an allocation of over thirty examples of the class.

In 1961 British Railways started to take delivery of the most powerful of its early diesel locomotives with the arrival of the English Electric Type 5 (Class 55) Deltics. Twenty-two of these had been ordered to replace steam traction working express passenger traffic on the East Coast Main Line, and six were based at Gateshead. Along with their classmates based at Finsbury Park and Haymarket they were soon handling all the major express passenger trains on the route and earned their keep in this way for nearly twenty years until replaced by InterCity 125 High Speed Trains. They were reliable and successful, and, despite their high maintenance costs, proved themselves worthy successors to the steam locomotives they replaced. Six examples have been acquired by preservation groups.

From May 1962 Gateshead depot also received twenty-eight examples of the BR/Sulzer Type 4 'Peak' (Class 46) with numbers D166 to D193 arriving ex-works and being allocated

Thursday 5 June 1958. With the opening of the new Thornaby locomotive depot on this day, we see here the Officers Special at Thornaby station with Brush Type 2 (Class 30) no. D5510 in charge. It is in virtually ex-works condition having entered service only a few days earlier. *(K.H. Cockerill/ARPT)*

to Inter-Regional expresses primarily between Newcastle and Liverpool. As the 1960s progressed, further designs of main line classes started to be delivered from manufacturers. English Electric Type 3 (Class 37) locomotives were being allocated to Hull Dairycoates depot from March 1962 onward and from September of the same year to Thornaby depot. This highly successful class of locomotives were to be found all over the North Eastern Region handling goods traffic. During 1964 examples of the final batch of Clayton Type 1 (Class 17) locomotives were being delivered from Beyer Peacock to Thornaby depot, they subsequently experienced the shortest working lives of any of the main line diesel classes with some examples being withdrawn only four years later and the final examples being withdrawn during 1971.

One of the most successful of the later designs started to appear from the manufacturer in the summer of 1962 with the arrival of the Brush/Sulzer Type 4 (Class 47) locomotives. With over 500 examples constructed over a five-year period these became widely allocated, the North Eastern Region initially receiving examples at York (50A) and Gateshead (52A). These were soon regarded as efficient and versatile workhorses handling all types of traffic from express passenger to fast fitted goods trains.

As part of the modernisation of the British Railways infrastructure, a new locomotive depot was opened at Thornaby on 5 June 1958. Occupying a 70-acre site this completely new depot incorporated a roundhouse structure for steam locomotives and dedicated diesel maintenance facilities – diesel locomotives being allocated there from its opening. Coded 51L, the new and expanded facilities there would allow the closure of four local steam sheds with Middlesbrough (51D) and Newport (51B) sheds closing during 1958 and Haverton Hill (51G) and Stockton (51E) closing during 1959 with locomotives based at these depots moving to the new shed. Thornaby depot was closed officially to steam traction during December 1964 but it continued as a diesel maintenance facility under the management of various companies. The steam roundhouse was demolished during 1988 with the diesel maintenance facilities continuing until finally being closed in 2007 with demolition following in 2011.

ACKNOWLEDGEMENTS

I particularly wish to thank Richard Barber of the Armstrong Railway Photographic Trust (ARPT) and Michael Mensing for their assistance with details for captioning. Thanks are also due to The National Railway Museum (NRM) for their approval to reproduce the photographs of Eric Treacy. Rob Fraser has been very helpful in sharing his encyclopaedic knowledge of British diesel traction. Other photographers have been credited where known and every effort has been made to trace copyright holders of photographs reproduced. Apologies are offered to any who may have been missed.

Sunday 19 July 1953. Painted in black, unlined livery and waiting to exit the paint shop at Darlington Works is one of the early batches of 350hp 0–6–0 diesel electric shunters (Class 08) constructed there. No. 13060 would become no. D3060 and finally 08 047 in TOPS, surviving until October 1979 before withdrawal from service. *(F.W. Hampson/ARPT)*

Saturday 5 September 1953. Inside the paint shop at Darlington Works again, this time with 350hp 0–6–0 diesel electric shunter (Class 08) no. 13064 in undercoat colour. Destined to become no. D3064, she would be numbered 08 051 in TOPS and was withdrawn almost thirty years later during July 1982. *(F.W. Hampson/ARPT)*

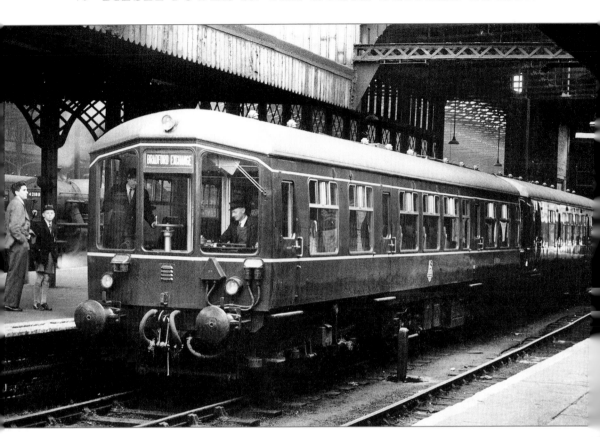

October 1954. Derby Works-constructed 'Lightweight' DMUs were beginning to arrive in the North Eastern Region for trial and this two-car set, seen approaching Billingham, has a suburban coach in tow. Note the use, still, of lamps indicating a class A working. *(J. Phillips/ARPT)*

Opposite top: **Wednesday 16 June 1954**. Three days after the commencement of the newly dieselised Leeds to Bradford local services, a two-car 'Derby Lightweight' DMU waits to depart from Leeds Central with a service to Bradford Exchange. Eight of these units were constructed by British Railways at Derby Works and were delivered in April 1954 for testing prior to entering revenue-earning service. Fitted with 125hp Leyland engines and Hydro Mechanical Torque Converters, they proved popular with the public and perfectly suitable for the traffic allocated to them. Unfortunately they were the only vehicles fitted with the 'Red Triangle' coupling code and therefore had a relatively short working life, all being withdrawn early in 1964. *(W.S. Garth)*

Opposite bottom: **Sunday 25 July 1954**. In ex-works condition NBL-constructed 200hp diesel hydraulic 0–4–0 shunter no. 11702 is standing outside Darlington Works having been delivered earlier in the month. It would become D2702 and it would be withdrawn during March 1967. *(M. Brown)*

September 1955. Seen standing outside Darlington Works is 350hp 0–6–0 diesel electric shunter no. 13161 having emerged from the works prior to entering service. This example was fitted with a Blackstone engine, it would be renumbered D3161 and was withdrawn in September 1967. *(R. Payne/ARPT)*

Opposite top: **Sunday 20 November 1955**. This photograph taken in the interior of Newcastle Central station shows a four-car 'Derby Lightweight' DMU preparing to depart on a service to South Shields. These four-car units formed part of the second delivery of DMUs from Derby Works, being introduced in November 1954. Fitted with 150hp AEC engines and Mechanical Pre-selector gearboxes, these were initially introduced to services in West Cumberland and later were seen, as here, on services in the Tyneside area. The units had a 'Yellow Diamond' coupling code and although incompatible with other DMUs saw much use well into the 1960s before being withdrawn. *(F. W. Hampson/ARPT)*

Opposite bottom: **Wednesday 11 April 1956**. Shunting in Hull Neptune Street Yard is 350hp 0–6–0 (Class 08) diesel electric shunter no. 13238. Constructed at Darlington Works in February 1956 it would be renumbered D3238 and survive to be given the number 08 170 in TOPS. It would be withdrawn from service in March 1986. Note the ex-private-owner, wooden bodied wagon still in use at this time, coupled next to the locomotive. *(Author's Collection)*

Wednesday 24 July 1957. Parked in a goods yard in Hull between duties is 350hp 0–6–0 diesel electric shunter (Class 08) no. 13234. A product of Darlington Works and entering service in January 1956 it would be numbered D3234 and later 08 166 in TOPS. It would be withdrawn from service during July 1982. *(Author's Collection)*

Opposite top: **Tuesday 3 September 1957**. On this day the interior of Darlington Works erecting shop has three 350hp 0–6–0 diesel electric shunters under construction. These particular locomotives have Lister Blackstone diesel engines with GEC electrical equipment. *(Author's Collection)*

Opposite bottom: **Sunday 6 October 1957**. Seen here at Darlington, diminutive 200hp diesel hydraulic 0–4–0 shunter no. 11701 was constructed by the NBL in Glasgow and entered service in November 1954. One of only eight members of the class built, it would eventually be numbered D2701 and was withdrawn in March 1967. *(B.K.B. Green)*

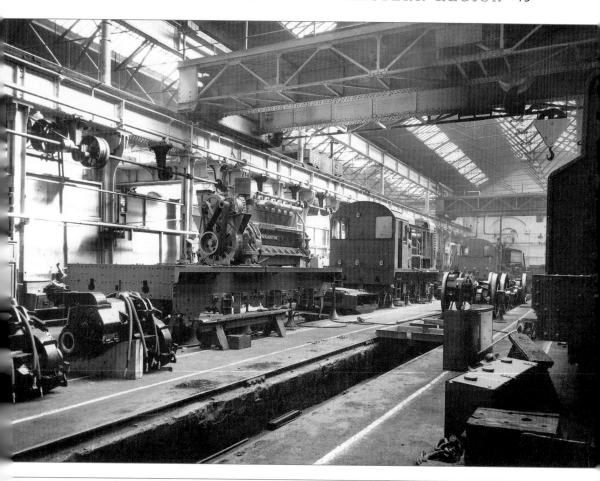

Wednesday 8 January 1958. Parked in the depot at Bradford Hammerton Street are the two newly constructed English Electric Type 1s (Class 20) nos D8010 and D8011. They had arrived for exhaust fume testing to take place. These two locomotives were constructed at the Vulcan Foundry and entered service in October and November 1957. They would be numbered 20 010 and 20 011 in TOPS with the former being withdrawn in December 1991 and the latter in February 1987. One of the early successes of the Pilot Scheme with 228 examples being constructed, many would still be in service with main line operators in the early years of the twenty-first century. A number of examples have also been purchased by preservation groups. *(G.W. Morrison)*

Sunday 19 January 1958. At Darlington MPD, 350hp 0–6–0 (Class 08) diesel electric shunter no. D3478 has just emerged from the works after completing construction but would not have a long service life, being withdrawn during June 1968. Note the use of the smaller capital letter 'D' prefix. *(A.W. Martin)*

Wednesday 5 March 1958. An interesting comparison of DMUs at Pontefract Monkhill station. On the left is a Metro-Cammell three-car set on a Bradford and Wakefield to Goole service. This is one of the units first introduced in October 1956 fitted with a two-character route indicator which would be designated Class 101 in TOPS. On the right is an original 'Derby Lightweight' two-car unit on a service to Leeds Central. *(T. Rounthwaite)*

April 1958. Two months into its service career, Brush-built Type 2 (Class 30) no. D5505 is seen parked in Doncaster depot yard. Initially allocated to Stratford depot, it would be re-engined during 1968 becoming Class 31 numbered 31 005 in TOPS and was withdrawn during February 1980. *(R.K. Evans)*

Monday 2 June 1958. Having been delivered from the Brush Works at Loughborough a few days earlier, Type 2 (Class 30) no. D5510 awaits commissioning at Doncaster Works. This early example is fitted with disc indicators but no doubt the next rostered crew will find the lamp useful. Re-engined during 1969, it would become Class 31 number 31 010 in TOPS. It would be withdrawn from service in July 1976. *(P. Tait)*

Opposite top: **April 1958**. Standing in the works yard at Doncaster is newly constructed 350hp 0–6–0 diesel electric (Class 08) shunter D3609. A product of Horwich Works during March of the same year, this locomotive would be numbered 08 494 and survive in service for over thirty years to be withdrawn in August 1988. *(R.K. Evans)*

Opposite bottom: **Sunday 20 April 1958**. Another ex-works 350hp 0–6–0 diesel electric (Class 08) shunter, no. D3655, is seen at Doncaster Works. A product of 'the plant' it also bears the smaller 'D' prefix and would eventually be numbered 08 500 in TOPS. By 2011 it would be owned by DB Schenker and held in store at Doncaster. *(B.K.B. Green)*

Sunday 13 July 1958. At this time the BRC&W Co. were constructing two-, three- and four-car DMUs which would be designated Class 104 in TOPS. This photograph, taken at Coldstream station, shows an afternoon excursion which had arrived from Newcastle via Berwick-upon-Tweed comprising two four-car sets incorporating car numbers 50545, 50546, 50566, 50567, 59191, 59192, 59212 and 59213 only recently delivered from the manufacturer. The train had departed Newcastle at 13.35 reaching Coldstream at 15.30, with a return to Berwick arriving at 17.25 and Newcastle at 21.47. The photographer noted that any prospective shoppers on the train would be disappointed as there would be no shops open in Coldstream on a Sunday and the return arrival time at Berwick meant that shops would be closing. The station at Coldstream was actually sited in England at the village of Cornhill-on-Tweed, a mere 1½ miles from Coldstream and the line from St Boswells to Tweedmouth would be closed to passenger traffic in June 1964. The station has since been demolished and a small housing estate constructed on the site. *(Howard Forster/ARPT)*

Opposite top: **Saturday 19 July 1958**. This summer scene at Middlesbrough station shows a five-car DMU formed by two-car and three-car Metro-Cammell units waiting to depart with the 13.28 service to Scarborough. The leading car of this unit (Class 101) is no. E56051 which has the extra third marker light above the destination blind. In the background, the public are being encouraged to 'Get Younger Here', a favourite slogan of the period used by the Edinburgh Brewers, William Younger. *(Michael Mensing)*

Opposite bottom: **Monday 21 July 1958**. Sitting in the long bay platform beside Falsgate signal-box at Scarborough station, is the 11.30 service to Middlesbrough comprising of a five-unit Metro-Cammell (Class 101) DMU formed by a two-car and a three-car set. The car nearest the camera is no. E50292. The signal-box, constructed in 1908, has weathered the test of time to become a grade II listed structure. It was due to be decommissioned at the end of 2010 along with the semaphore signals it controlled. *(Michael Mensing)*

Monday 21 July 1958. Seen here arriving at Whitby West Cliff station is the 08.02 Darlington to Scarborough service operated by a pair of three-car Metro-Cammell (Class 101) DMUs. Note the veteran lower quadrant slotted home signal at the platform end. *(Michael Mensing)*

Opposite top: **Monday 21 July 1958**. The 17.40 service to Middlesbrough waits to depart from Whitby Town station in the form of a two-car Derby-built (Class 108) unit coupled to a two-car Metro-Cammell (Class 101) unit. Introduced in May of this same year, construction of the Class 108 units continued until 1961 by which time over 300 cars had entered service. Powered by two Leyland 150hp engines and with a 'Blue Square' coupling code, these units would see service on the Eastern, North Eastern, London Midland and Scottish regions and it would be the early 1990s before they were withdrawn from main line service. *(Michael Mensing)*

Opposite bottom: **Tuesday 22 July 1958**. The background of this photograph contains the unmistakable outlines of the ruined abbey (right) and St Mary's Church (left) that sit above Whitby, both buildings being mentioned in the Bram Stoker novel *Dracula* published in 1897. In the foreground a three-car Metro-Cammell (Class 101) DMU is seen passing Bog Hall signal-box with the 16.30 service from Scarborough to Middlesbrough. *(Michael Mensing)*

Wednesday 23 July 1958. This busy scene is at Whitby Town station with a three-car Metro-Cammell (Class 101) DMU departing with the 16.30 Middlesbrough to Scarborough service, while on the left ex-LNER Class B1 4–6–0 no. 61071 waits to depart with the 18.10 to York service and Class L1 2–6–4 tank no. 67754 waits to depart with the 18.00 train to Middlesbrough. *(Michael Mensing)*

Opposite top: **Wednesday 23 July 1958**. The five-car 16.05 Whitby to Middlesbrough service, comprising two-unit and three-unit Metro-Cammell (Class 101) DMUs, has car no. E50186 leading as it is seen near Ruswarp station. *(Michael Mensing)*

Opposite bottom: **Wednesday 23 July 1958**. This three-car Metro-Cammell (Class 101) DMU is seen approaching Ruswarp station with the 16.30 service from Middlesbrough to Scarborough. This is one of the earlier members of the class fitted with four marker lights and destination blind. *(Michael Mensing)*

Sunday 27 July 1958. Having reversed at Whitby Town station, the 08.50 Scarborough to Darlington service is seen approaching Whitby West Cliff station. The leading car of this Metro-Cammell six-car (Class 101) DMU is no. E50260. *(Michael Mensing)*

Opposite top: **Thursday 24 July 1958**. This three-car Metro-Cammell (Class 101) DMU is seen entering Hayburn Wyke station with the 14.10 service from Scarborough to Whitby Town. This is one of the later members of the class fitted with two marker lights and a two-character route indicator. *(Michael Mensing)*

Opposite bottom: **Thursday 24 July 1958**. This six-car DMU is formed from two three-car Metro-Cammell (Class 101) sets and is operating the 19.10 Scarborough to Darlington service as it enters Ruswarp station. The leading car is no. E50261. *(Michael Mensing)*

Monday 28 July 1958. The 12.18 Redcar to Newcastle service is seen departing Middlesbrough station formed by two four-car Metro-Cammell (Class 101) DMUs. *(Michael Mensing)*

Opposite top: **Monday 28 July 1958**. This four-car Metro-Cammell (Class 101) DMU is awaiting its driver prior to departing from Darlington station with the 13.40 service to Richmond. *(Michael Mensing)*

Opposite bottom: **Friday 1 August 1958**. The 10.15 service from Scarborough to Middlesbrough is seen here approaching Grosmont station being operated by a two- and four-car unit of Metro-Cammell (Class 101) DMUs. *(Michael Mensing)*

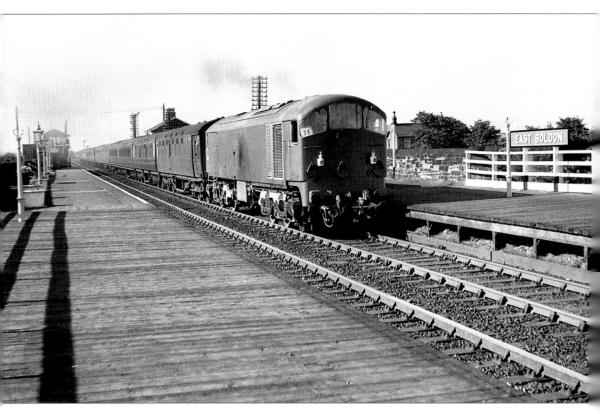

Sunday 1 March 1959. This Metro-Cammell (Class 101) DMU is sitting in the bay platform, 1A, at Scarborough station having just arrived with a service from Middlesbrough. *(N.W. Skinner/ARPT)*

Opposite top: **Saturday 16 August 1958**. The Metropolitan-Vickers Type 2 (Class 28) locomotives were unusual in having a Crossley V8 two-stroke diesel engine and a Co-Bo wheel arrangement which was unique in the UK. Constructed in their works at Stockton-on-Tees, the twenty locomotives built were road tested locally and here we see no. D5702, still in works primer, hauling a thirteen-coach test train as it passes through East Boldon station. The class proved to be unreliable and all were withdrawn by 1969, no. D5702 coming out of service during September 1968. One example, no. D5705, survived into the preservation scene and is to be found at the East Lancashire Railway. East Boldon station is now used by the Tyne and Wear Metro trains but no main line services stop at the station. *(I.S. Carr/ARPT)*

Opposite bottom: **September 1958**. This service from York to Hull is seen passing Cottingham South signal-box as it approaches Cottingham station. Operated by two two-car Cravens-built (Class 105) DMUs, these were first introduced in 1956 utilising AEC 150hp engines and were 'Blue Square' coupling coded. Initially fitted with four marker lights and a destination blind, later units of this class were constructed with a two-character route indicator on the cab front. The station, opened by the Hull and Selby Railway in 1846, is still used by Northern Rail services from Hull to Bridlington and Scarborough. *(B. Todd)*

Sunday 8 March 1959. Seen here at Doncaster, this 204hp diesel mechanical (Class 03) 0–6–0 shunter, no. D2083, is in ex-works condition having just emerged from the works where it was constructed. It would only survive ten years before withdrawal in June 1969. *(A.W. Martin)*

Thursday 21 May 1959. This bright spring day at Thirsk sees a six-car train made up of three 'Derby Lightweight' two-car units working a stopping service to York. The first car, no. E79139, has by now acquired the speed whiskers motif. These units were from the second introduction in November 1954 which used the yellow diamond coupling code. *(Brian Morrison)*

Friday 22 May 1959. Having just departed Harrogate station, this Metro-Cammell three-car (Class 101) DMU is seen on a service to Bradford Exchange. The leading car, no. E50170, is in original as built condition and has yet to acquire the speed whiskers motif. *(Brian Morrison)*

Monday 25 May 1959. With delivery mileage only on the clock, Brush Type 2 (Class 30) no. D5531 awaits commissioning in Doncaster Works yard. This example has the cab roof-mounted four-character route indicator – earlier examples were fitted with disc indicators. Re-engined during 1968 it would be withdrawn after almost forty years' service in February 1999, numbered 31 113 in TOPS. *(Brian Morrison)*

Sunday 31 May 1959. One of the early successes of the Modernisation Report Pilot Scheme was the English Electric-built Type 4 locomotives that would become designated Class 40 in TOPS. Seen here is one of the first batch constructed, no. D206, entering Knottingley at the head of the 10.40 ex-Newcastle. Built at the Vulcan Foundry and entering service in July 1958, it would be numbered 40 006 and would be withdrawn from service during March 1983. *(Kenneth Field)*

June 1959. This Metro-Cammell-built two-unit (Class 101) DMU is seen departing from Goldsborough station while working a Harrogate to York service. The platforms at this station were staggered with one on either side of the road crossing. Note the slotted lower quadrant home signal paired with an upper quadrant subsidiary signal. The station would be closed to traffic only three months after this photograph was taken. *(Peter Sunderland)*

Saturday 4 July 1959. This photograph shows the approach to Darlington station from the north with a two-car Metro-Cammell (Class 101) DMU approaching with a service from Barnard Castle. *(A. Abbott)*

Monday 26 October 1959. Pausing at Hexham station, the 06.50 Newcastle to Carlisle parcels train is headed by English Electric Type 4 no. D237 in ex-works condition. This locomotive is probably undertaking driver training turns as it was only delivered a few days earlier to Gateshead depot. This was the first of eleven examples of the type to be allocated to Gateshead. It would be withdrawn from service during August 1981 numbered 40 037. *(M.S. Kington)*

Saturday 20 February 1960. Seen here gathering speed while heading the 12.05 Newcastle to Colchester train is English Electric Type 4 (Class 40) no. D251 passing Villette Road 'box. Note the mixture of coaching stock with Gresley, Thompson and BR Mark 1 coaches in the rake. Another example of the type allocated to Gateshead, this locomotive was a product of the Vulcan Foundry, entering service in December 1959. It would be renumbered 40 051 and was withdrawn from service during January 1978. *(S.E. Teasdale)*

Opposite top: **Monday 30 May 1960**. English Electric Type 4 (Class 40) no. D240 is seen here at the head of a London King's Cross to Glasgow express departing York station. Note the Minster, partly clad in scaffolding, in the background. Introduced to service in October 1959 and allocated to Gateshead, this locomotive would be withdrawn during July 1980 numbered 40 040. *(L. Metcalfe)*

Opposite bottom: **Tuesday 26 July 1960**. This Northallerton to Starbeck goods train is seen passing Wormald Green headed by 350hp 0–6–0 (Class 08) shunter no. D3319. Built at Darlington Works in October 1956 it was originally numbered 13319 and it would be withdrawn in May 1985 numbered 08 249. Note the use of the smaller 'D' prefix. *(R. Leslie/ARPT)*

Saturday 30 July 1960. Speeding past Croft Spa is English Electric Type 4 (Class 40) no. D259 at the head of the Up 'Queen of Scots Pullman'. This train service had been introduced by the LNER in 1928 to replace the 'Harrogate Pullman' which ran from King's Cross to Leeds and Harrogate. The new service ran not only to these two cities but was extended to Edinburgh Waverley and Glasgow Queen Street and continued until the spring of 1964. It was replaced by the 'White Rose Pullman' which ran between King's Cross and Leeds. The locomotive, which entered service in February 1960 and was allocated to York depot, would be numbered 40 059 in TOPS and was withdrawn during August 1977. *(R. Leslie/ARPT)*

Monday 15 August 1960. In June 1875 the branch from Melmerby to Masham was opened by the North Eastern Railway to serve this ancient market town famous for its sheep markets. In later years it became well known for the Theakstons Brewery which had been established in 1827. The branch was closed to passenger traffic in January 1931 but goods traffic continued until November 1963 when the line was closed completely. Here we see the daily goods train hauled by 350hp 0–6–0 (Class 08) shunter no. D3313 negotiating the Millbank crossing. This locomotive was a product of Darlington Works, entering service in June 1956, and it was originally numbered 13313. It appears to have been withdrawn towards the end of 1985 numbered 08 243. *(R.E. James-Robertson)*

Sunday 16 October 1960. BR/Sulzer Type 2 (Class 24) no. D5103 at Darlington. A product of Darlington Works in August of the same year, it was one of a batch of seven examples of the type allocated new to Gateshead depot. It would be numbered 24 103 and was withdrawn during December 1976. *(P.H. Wells)*

March 1961. Emerging from the gloomy interior of York station, English Electric Type 4 (Class 40) no. D201, by this time allocated to Finsbury Park depot, is hauling the Down 'Flying Scotsman'. One of the first batch of ten locomotives of the class constructed by them at their Vulcan Foundry works in April 1958 it would be numbered 40 001 in TOPS and was withdrawn in April 1984. *(Dr P. Ransome-Wallis)*

Saturday 20 May 1961. This Down excursion, seen at Mere near Scarborough, is in the hands of Brush Type 2 (Class 30) no. D5693. Coming into service in March 1961 and re-engined during 1967, this locomotive would be withdrawn during October 1994 numbered 31 263. *(N.W. Skinner/ARPT)*

Opposite top: **Thursday 16 March 1961**. English Electric Type 4 (Class 40) no. D249 is seen here departing Leeds City station with the 09.45 Newcastle to Liverpool service. Another Gateshead-allocated locomotive entering service in November 1959, it would be withdrawn in January 1983 numbered 40 049. *(G.W. Morrison)*

Opposite bottom: **Wednesday 5 April 1961**. Sitting within Leeds City station is BR/Sulzer 'Peak' Type 4 (class 45) no. D92. This was a product of Crewe Works and had entered service only a few days earlier so was probably still completing running in duties. It would be numbered 45 138 in TOPS and withdrawn from service in December 1986. *(Michael Roberts)*

Thursday 9 July 1961. Parked in the yard at Darlington depot is 204hp diesel mechanical 0–6–0 (Class 05) shunter no. D2587. Built by Hunslet in November 1959 it would be withdrawn during December 1967 and sold into industrial use. It survived until 1980 when it was finally sold into the preservation scene where it is currently based at the East Lancashire Railway. *(R.A. Panting)*

Opposite top: **Tuesday 20 June 1961**. This BRC&W three-car DMU was one of only thirty sets constructed primarily for the 'Calder Valley' route services which were introduced during the month this photograph was taken. It is seen in ex-works condition as it enters York station from the south on a trial run. Under TOPS these units would be designated Class 110. Equipped with 180hp Rolls-Royce engines and fitted with standard mechanical transmission these powerful units were 'Blue Square' coupling coded. Many of the cars continued in service until the early 1990s. *(S. Creer)*

Opposite bottom: **Tuesday 27 June 1961**. Awaiting its next duty at Leeds City station is BR/Sulzer 'Peak' Type 4 (class 45) no. D31. This locomotive was constructed at Derby Works and entered service earlier in the same month. It became numbered 45 030 in TOPS and was withdrawn from service in November 1980. *(G.W. Morrison)*

Saturday 29 July 1961. Seen here working an Up special passing Seamer East 'box is Sheffield (Darnall) resident Brush Type 2 (Class 30) no. D5690. Only four months old, this locomotive would be re-engined during 1967 and would see just over twenty-two years' service before being withdrawn in May 1983 numbered 31 262 in TOPS. *(P.H. Wells)*

Sunday 6 August 1961. The headcode on English Electric Type 4 (Class 40) no. D244 indicates an empty coaching stock working and the train is formed of approximately twenty assorted parcels vans and coaches. The diesel is assisting ex-LNER Class B1 4-6-0 no. 61071 as they move this York to Manchester train up Micklefield Bank. *(M. Mitchell)*

Monday 21 August 1961. The 13.00 Darlington to Sunderland service is in the hands of a two-car Metro-Cammell (Class 101) DMU. It is seen taking the Leamside line at Newtonhall signal-box. *(I.S. Carr/ARPT)*

Wednesday 23 August 1961. English Electric Type 4 (Class 40) no. D308 is seen entering Huddersfield station with a Liverpool to Newcastle passenger train. This locomotive was one of the twenty examples of the class constructed at the Robert Stephenson and Hawthorn Works, entering service in November 1960. It would be withdrawn in August 1980 numbered 40 108 in TOPS. *(R.J. Blenkinsop)*

Wednesday 14 March 1962. This Up test train comprising ten suburban coaches, and being hauled by a rather dirty looking English Electric Type 4 (Class 40), no. D253, is approaching Wortley Junction, Leeds. The tall tower in the background is part of the Albion Works owned by Greenwood & Batley Ltd who produced electric and battery/electric locomotives for the mining industry and electric platform trolleys using their famous trade name 'Greenbat'. By 1984 the company was closed and 1987 saw the site completely closed and the bulk of the buildings demolished. The locomotive was constructed in January 1960 and initially allocated to York depot. It would be renumbered 40 053 and was withdrawn from service during August 1976. *(G.W. Morrison)*

Opposite top: **Saturday 23 September 1961**. The annual North Tyneside Agricultural Show held at Bellingham was one of the largest in Northumberland, so much so that BR continued to run a special train from Newbiggin and Morpeth to Bellingham via Reedsmouth over the ex-NBR 'Border Counties' route which had been closed to regular passenger traffic in 1952. Looking north at Reedsmouth, the line to Bellingham and Riccarton Junction is on the left and the line from Scotsgap and Morpeth to the right. The train had to reverse at Reedsmouth to reach Bellingham, as the photograph shows, and in 1961 this consisted of an eight-car DMU formed by a four-car Derby-built (Class 108) set and a four-car Metro-Cammell (Class 101) set that departed Newbiggin at 08.51. The two impressive buildings on the platform, the signal-box and water tower, have both been converted into houses. Founded and run since 1842, the annual show is still one of the largest in Northern England. *(W.S. Sellar)*

Opposite bottom: **Wednesday 10 January 1962**. At Harrogate station a comparison can be made between two types of similar DMUs. On the left is a BRC&W three-car set introduced in 1961 initially for the 'Calder Valley' route services. These units would be designated Class 110 in TOPS. On the right is an earlier DMU Class 104 from the same manufacturer, a two-car unit first introduced in 1957 waiting to depart with a service to Darlington. *(P.J. Sharpe)*

Saturday 24 March 1962. This long-distance working from Cliffe in Kent to Uddingston in Scotland comprises twenty-six cement tankers and is seen approaching York being hauled by a pair of BRC&W Type 3s (Class 33), no. D6553 leading no. D6570. The former entered service in May 1961 with the latter following in September of the same year. Both locomotives have managed to find their way into the preservation scene with the first being withdrawn in October 1996 numbered 33 035 and is now to be found at Barrow Hill undergoing restoration. The second locomotive was withdrawn in February 1997 numbered 33 052 in TOPS and is now based at the Kent and East Sussex Railway. *(P.J. Lynch)*

Friday 30 March 1962. BRC&W-built Type 2 (Class 27) no. D5375 heads a C class goods train at Boroughbridge Road, Northallerton. Entering service in the month prior to this photograph the locomotive would be withdrawn during August 1984 numbered 27 028. *(G.W. Morrison)*

Friday 13 April 1962. This Morecambe to Leeds passenger train is seen passing Saltaire with BR/Sulzer 'Peak' Type 4 (Class 46) no. D151 in charge. A product of Derby Works in January of the same year, it would be numbered 46 014 in TOPS and withdrawn during May 1984. The station was closed in March 1965 but reopened during April 1984 as an unstaffed halt to serve Northern Rail trains on the Leeds, Bradford and Skipton commuter traffic. *(G.W. Morrison)*

Friday 13 April 1962. On this 'Friday 13th' a pair of BRC&W Type 2s (Class 27) have drawn the short straw and are seen working a class 7 Down train of iron ore wagons. No. D5371 is leading sister no. D5372. Both locomotives entered service in January 1962 with the former, renumbered 27 025, being withdrawn during June 1987 and the latter, renumbered 27 026, being withdrawn a month later in July 1987. *(P.J. Lynch)*

Friday 4 May 1962. In sparkling ex-works condition, English Electric Type 3 (Class 37) no. D6736 sits beside a classmate at Thornaby depot. Built at the Vulcan Foundry and introduced only a few days earlier, this locomotive would be allocated new to Hull Dairycoates. By 1977 it would be working out of March depot and during 1985 it was based at Cardiff Canton. In TOPS it would be numbered 37 036, then 37 507 and finally 37 605 and by 2011 it would be owned by Direct Rail Services and held in store at Carnforth. *(David Dippie/ARPT)*

Saturday 19 May 1962. The as yet to be named English Electric Deltic Type 5 (Class 55) no. D9010 is accelerating through the centre road at York station while in charge of the Down 'Flying Scotsman'. Constructed at the Vulcan Foundry and introduced to service in July 1961 it was allocated to Haymarket depot in Edinburgh and it would be May 1965 before it acquired the name *The King's Own Scottish Borderer* during a ceremony at Dumfries station. The locomotive would be withdrawn in December 1981 numbered 55 010. *(Michael Mensing)*

Saturday 19 May 1962. BR/Sulzer 'Peak' Type 4 (Class 45) no. D108 has arrived at York station with the 06.43 Gloucester (Eastgate) to York service and one of the locomotive crew is overseeing the taking of water for the train heating boiler. The locomotive, sporting a 17A Derby shed code plate, was constructed at Crewe Works in July 1961 and would be withdrawn during July 1988 numbered 45 012. *(Michael Mensing)*

Saturday 19 May 1962. This splendid photograph shows the 11.35 Newcastle to Leeds (City) service pausing under the magnificent roof structure at York station. The leading four cars of this six-car set are from the second delivery of 'Derby Lightweight' DMUs which entered service in November 1954. The leading car is no. E79152. *(Michael Mensing)*

Tuesday 22 May 1962. On this clear spring morning, English Electric Type 4 (Class 40) no. D266 is seen departing the north sidings at Berwick-upon-Tweed with a northbound goods train. This was one of seven examples of the type allocated new to Haymarket depot in Edinburgh. Entering service in March 1960 and numbered 40 066 in TOPS, it would be withdrawn during April 1981. *(Michael Mensing)*

Opposite top: **Saturday 19 May 1962**. Another Brush-built Type 2 (Class 30), no. D5841, is awaiting commissioning in Doncaster Works yard. This later example has both the four-character cab mounted route indicator and a small yellow warning panel. Re-engined in 1965 it would be withdrawn as no. 31 308 in TOPS during August 1999. *(Brian Stephenson)*

Opposite bottom: **Sunday 20 May 1962**. The 20.05 Edinburgh Waverley to London King's Cross passenger train has arrived at Berwick-upon-Tweed behind English Electric Type 4 (Class 40) no. D245 and the crew are waiting for the 'right of way' before proceeding south. Coming into service during November 1959 and allocated to Gateshead, this locomotive would be numbered 40 045 and was withdrawn in August 1976. *(Michael Mensing)*

Monday 28 May 1962. At Manors station, Newcastle, English Electric Type 4 (Class 40) no. D245 is working the 10.20 Edinburgh to Newcastle stopping service. *(Michael Mensing)*

Opposite top: **Wednesday 23 May 1962**. Near Marshall Meadows, just north of Berwick-upon-Tweed, English Electric Type 4 (Class 40) no. D249 is seen with an Up fitted goods. *(Michael Mensing)*

Opposite bottom: **Thursday 24 May 1962**. Hurrying north at the head of the Down 'Heart of Midlothian' London to Edinburgh service, English Electric Deltic Type 5 (Class 55) no. D9012 *Crepello* is approaching Tweedmouth. Arriving ex-works in September 1961 the locomotive was named at Doncaster Works prior to entering service and allocated to Finsbury Park depot in London. It would be withdrawn in May 1981 numbered 55 012. The 'Heart of Midlothian' service was a post-war introduction in 1951 which would cease operation in 1968. *(Michael Mensing)*

Thursday 31 May 1962. Seen here near Beal, south of Berwick-upon-Tweed, is English Electric Type 4 (Class 40) no. D272 as it speeds south with a fitted goods train. Another Gateshead-allocated locomotive coming into service in April 1960, it would be numbered 40 072 in TOPS and was withdrawn during August 1977. *(Michael Mensing)*

Opposite top: **Tuesday 29 May 1962**. English Electric Type 4 (Class 40) no. D348 is in charge of the Down 'Queen of Scots Pullman' car train as it approaches Alnmouth station. Entering service during June 1961 and allocated initially to Leeds Neville Hill depot, the locomotive would be withdrawn in August 1982 numbered 40 148. *(Michael Mensing)*

Opposite bottom: **Tuesday 29 May 1962**. This Metro-Cammell two-car (Class 101) DMU is waiting to depart Newcastle station with a service to Alnwick. The leading car is no. E56073. The branch from Alnmouth, on the East Coast Main Line, to Alnwick was closed to passenger traffic in January 1968. Goods traffic ceased in October of the same year and the track was removed shortly afterwards. *(Michael Mensing)*

Friday 1 June 1962. This splendid photograph shows English Electric Type 4 (Class 40) no. D244, bearing a 52A Gateshead shed code plate, preparing to depart York station with a Glasgow to London King's Cross passenger train. Entering service during November 1959 this locomotive would be allocated to Gateshead depot and withdrawn in January 1985 numbered 40 044. *(F. Wilde)*

Monday 11 June 1962. English Electric Type 4 (Class 40) no. D244 waits to depart from Hull Paragon station at the head of a parcels train. *(I.S. Carr/ARPT)*

Opposite top: **Saturday 9 June 1962**. Waiting to depart Hull Paragon station at the head of the 16.30 passenger train to Doncaster, Sheffield Victoria and Liverpool Central is Brush-built Type 3 (Class 30) no. D5656. Entering service during October 1960 this locomotive would be re-engined in 1968 and withdrawn over thirty years later in January 1991 numbered 31 409 in TOPS. *(I S Carr/ARPT)*

Opposite bottom: **Saturday 9 June 1962**. English Electric Type 3 no. D6739 is seen waiting to depart from Hull Paragon station with the 17.17 passenger train to London King's Cross via Doncaster. In ex-works condition and only a few days into its service career, she would be numbered 37 039, then 37 504 and finally 37 603 and is, fifty years later, still in main line service with Direct Rail Services. *(I.S. Carr/ARPT)*

Tuesday 12 June 1962. This train consisting of two two-car Cravens-built DMUs forms a service bound for Withernsea, seen here passing West Parade 'box in Hull. This is the earlier form of what was to become designated Class 105 in TOPS fitted with four marker lights and a destination blind.
(I.S. Carr/ARPT)

Tuesday 12 June 1962. The Botanic Gardens DMU depot in Hull is seen here packed with an assortment of DMUs constructed by different manufacturers including Cravens, BRC&W and Metro-Cammell.
(I.S. Carr/ARPT)

Tuesday 12 June 1962. This Cravens two-car (Class 105) DMU is working a Hull to Hornsea service seen here between West Parade signal-box and Botanic Gardens. *(I.S. Carr/ARPT)*

Tuesday 12 June 1962. Another Cravens-built two-car (Class 105) DMU here seen working the 11.00 service to Hull departing from Goole station. The leading car, no. E56130, has by now lost its speed whiskers motif and is sporting a small yellow panel. *(I.S. Carr/ARPT)*

Tuesday 12 June 1962. This is a rear view of a BRC&W (Class 104) DMU as it passes near West Parade 'box, Hull, operating a service to Beverley. The train is seen crossing the lines that enable through-running between Hessle and Botanic Gardens. *(I.S. Carr/ARPT)*

Opposite top: **Wednesday 13 June 1962**. Speeding through the centre roads at Hessle station is the 08.57 Nottingham Midland to Hull service. This is being operated by a pair of two-car Derby Works-constructed DMUs which were designated Class 114 in TOPS. Introduced in late 1956 these units were powered by 230hp Leyland engines and were at first allocated to the Eastern region. Many of the units survived in service until the early 1990s before the last of the class was withdrawn. *(I.S. Carr/ARPT)*

Opposite bottom: **Wednesday 13 June 1962**. A Swindon-built 'Trans-Pennine' (Class 124) six-car DMU is seen here working the 07.50 Liverpool Lime Street to Hull service at Brough station. Originally all based at Leeds Neville Hill depot, these units would eventually be allocated to the Botanic Gardens depot in Hull after its refurbishment as a dedicated diesel maintenance facility. *(I.S. Carr/ARPT)*

Saturday 16 June 1962. This view is of the rear of the last regular passenger train from Bishop Auckland to Barnard Castle and it is seen negotiating the sharp curve to West Auckland. The seven-car service consists of three-car and four-car Metro-Cammell (Class 101) DMUs. Note the splendid gantry with its array of NER lower quadrant signals. *(M. Dunnett)*

Opposite top: **Saturday 21 July 1962**. The 13.26 service from Sunderland to Durham consisting of a two-car BRC&W (class 104) unit coupled between two two-car Metro-Cammell (Class 101) units, climbs out of Sunderland to Fawcett Street Junction on this Durham Miners Gala Day. *(I.S. Carr/ARPT)*

Opposite bottom: **August 1962**. This Down goods train has just passed Greatham station heading for Newcastle behind BR/Sulzer Type 2 (Class 25) no. D5152. In the left background is the imposing Cerebos Salt Works at Greatham. Founded in 1874 to extract salt using brine pumps, this factory finally ceased producing salt in 1970/1. The locomotive was a product of Darlington Works that entered service during May 1961 and would be numbered 25 002. It was withdrawn in December 1980. The station would be closed to passenger traffic in November 1991. *(J. Appleton)*

Friday 3 August 1962. Having just traversed York station, English Electric Type 4 (Class 40) no. D356 is seen here working an Up goods train. Introduced to service a year earlier, it would be numbered 40 156 and was withdrawn during July 1980. *(R.A. Panting)*

Saturday 4 August 1962. BR/Sulzer Type 2 (Class 24) no. D5111, bearing a 52A Gateshead shed code, is working the 09.55 (SO) Whitley Bay to Glasgow service seen here coming off the Bedlington branch at Morpeth. This branch lost its passenger services in April 1950. The locomotive had been constructed at Darlington Works in November 1960 and would be withdrawn during February 1976 numbered 24 111. The train was taken forward to Glasgow by Class A2/3 4–6–2 no. 60517 *Ocean Swell* whose tender can be seen just to the left of the water column. *(R.G. Warwick)*

Monday 6 August 1962. This train comprising two two-car Derby-built (Class 108) DMUs is the 14.00 Ilkley to Leeds City service seen here between Ilkley and Rhydding. Introduced in May 1958, this photograph shows the original cab fronts with two marker lights, destination blind and a two-character route indicator. Later units would be fitted with a four-character route indicator on the cab roof. *(R.C. Browne)*

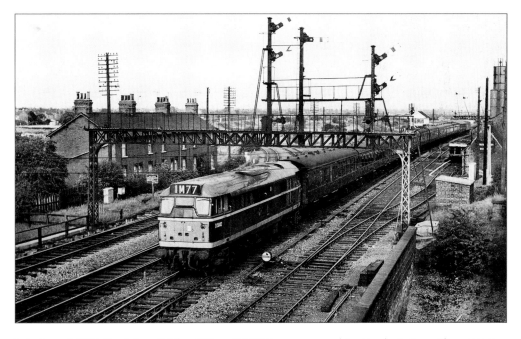

Late August 1962. Brush Type 2 (Class 30) no. D5842 is seen approaching Hessle station with a passenger train. The headcode would indicate a Liverpool service. Beginning its service career in May of the same year, it would be re-engined during 1967 becoming a Class 31 numbered 31 416 then 31 516 in TOPS before being withdrawn during October 1995. *(Author's Collection)*

Early September 1962. Trundling through the centre roads at Hessle station towards Hull with a class 8 mineral train is Brush Type 2 (Class 30) no. D5846. At this time the locomotive was allocated to Sheffield Darnall, 41A. Only three months old it would be re-engined in 1965 and become one of the longest-serving members of the class, being withdrawn from main line duties in March 1996 numbered 31 312. *(J.D. Walker)*

September 1962. By now sporting a small yellow warning panel on its nose, English Electric Type 4 (Class 40) no. D279 is seen departing West Hartlepool with a Newcastle to Liverpool express. Constructed during June 1960 this locomotive would be another of Gateshead's allocation and was withdrawn in January 1985 numbered 40 079. *(J. Appleton)*

Sunday 23 September 1962. This 204hp diesel mechanical 0–6–0 (Class 05) shunter no. D2604 is looking rather careworn at Darlington depot. Missing some brake blocks and coupling rods it presumably is undergoing some maintenance. It was a product of the Hunslet Works in September 1960 and it would be withdrawn during December 1967. *(A.W. Martin)*

Saturday 29 September 1962. Glistening in the summer sunshine at Doncaster Works are two ex-works English Electric Type 3 (Class 37) locomotives. No. D6775 is closest to the camera and it sits buffered up to no. D6755. The former was a product of the Robert Stephenson and Hawthorn Works and its first allocation was to Thornaby depot. By 1987 it would be working out of Stratford depot and by November 1999 it would be withdrawn numbered 37 075 and sold to a preservation group. It can currently be seen at the Churnet Valley Railway. The latter locomotive had been constructed at the Vulcan Foundry and also went new to Thornaby depot. It would be withdrawn almost forty-six years later in February 2008 numbered 37 055. *(John K. Morton)*

Tuesday 19 March 1963. BR/Sulzer Type 2 (Class 24) no. D5112, coupled to a brake tender, is seen waiting to depart from the ICI works at Billingham with a train of chemical tankers heading for Middlesbrough dock. Another Darlington-constructed locomotive from December 1960, it would be withdrawn during December 1976 numbered 24 112. *(Author's Collection)*

Opposite top: **Saturday 3 November 1962**. English Electric Type 3s (Class 37) newly allocated to Thornaby were making more journeys on the route to Leeds. Seen here at Bardsey is no. D6755 working with a brake tender on the morning Teeside to Neville Hill steel train. *(J.M. Rayner)*

Opposite bottom: **Thursday 7 March 1963**. This three-car Metro-Cammell (Class 111) DMU is seen entering Dewsbury (Wellington Road) with a service to Huddersfield. This class was introduced in April 1957 with some later units incorporating the very prominent four-character headcode panel. Powered by Rolls-Royce 180hp engines, the class was finally withdrawn from main line service in the late 1980s. *(J.S. Whiteley)*

Monday 29 April 1963. In this unusual photograph, the driver and secondman of English Electric Deltic Type 5 no. D9017 appear to be struggling in an attempt to fill the steam heating water tank using the water crane at the end of the platform at Stockton station while operating the 10.00 London King's Cross to Edinburgh service. The locomotive entered service during November 1961 and would be allocated to Gateshead depot. It was named *The Durham Light Infantry* at a ceremony at Durham station on 29 October 1963 and would eventually be numbered 55 017 and withdrawn in December 1981. *(I.S. Carr/ARPT)*

Opposite top: **Monday 27 May 1963**. BR/Sulzer Type 2 (Class 25) no. D5176 waits to depart Leeds City station light engine having worked in with the 10.38 Bradford Forster Square to Leeds section of 'The Devonian' restaurant car express to Paignton in Devon. This locomotive was constructed at Darlington Works and entered service during January 1963. She would be withdrawn numbered 25 026 in November 1980. 'The Devonian', introduced in 1927, ran from Bradford and Leeds via Sheffield, Derby, Birmingham, Cheltenham and Bristol to Paignton taking nine hours to complete the journey. The service would be withdrawn during 1975. *(R.F. Roberts/SLS)*

Opposite bottom: **Monday 3 June 1963**. Brush-built Type 2 (Class 30) no. D5858 is seen here working a returning race day special from Wetherby to Heeley (near Sheffield) as it approaches Thorner. Built during September 1962, re-engined in 1967, it would be numbered 31 323 and withdrawn in June 1989. *(M. Mitchell)*

Saturday 22 June 1963. The enthusiasts at the south end of York station are showing little interest in the departure of this four-car BRC&W (Class 104) DMU with car no. E50586 leading. The speed whisker motif has been replaced by a small yellow warning panel. *(C. W.R. Bowman)*

Opposite top: **Monday 3 June 1963**. Near Thorner again, we see the 15.00 Liverpool to Newcastle passenger train being hauled by BR/Sulzer 'Peak' Type 4 (Class 46) no. D171. Built at Derby Works in July 1962 it would be withdrawn during December 1980 numbered 46 034. *(M. Mitchell)*

Opposite bottom: **Saturday 8 June 1963**. With the Uddingston to Cliffe cement tanks in tow, BRC&W Type 3 (Class 33) no. D6555 approaches York. Built in May 1961 it would be withdrawn during September 1987 numbered 33 037. *(P.J. Lynch)*

Sunday 21 July 1963. Brush Type 4 (Class 47) no. D1522 is seen passing Wapping Bridge signal-box, between Penshaw and Fence Houses with the 10.10 Edinburgh to London King's Cross service. Only a month old, this locomotive would be numbered 47 002 in TOPS and withdrawn during June 1991. *(I.S. Carr/ARPT)*

Opposite top: **Thursday 4 July 1963.** This three-car Metro-Cammell (Class 101) DMU is seen entering Ravenscar station with the 16.25 Scarborough to Middlesbrough service. This unit was one of the later introductions with a two-character route indicator. *(R.F. Roberts/SLS)*

Opposite bottom: **Saturday 20 July 1963.** Parked near the site of the former engine shed at Durham North, English Electric Type 3 (Class 37) no. D6795 has been allocated as relief engine for any failures to other locomotives throughout this Durham Miners Gala Day. This example of the class was constructed at the Robert Stephenson and Hawthorn Works of English Electric during March 1963. It would be numbered 37 095 and was withdrawn in January 1999. *(I.S. Carr/ARPT)*

Saturday 27 July 1963. BR/Sulzer Type 2 (Class 25) no. D5171 comes off the Waterhouses branch at Dearness Valley 'box with an excursion from Ushaw Moor to Redcar. The Waterhouses branch had lost its passenger services during October 1951. A product of Darlington Works during January 1962, this locomotive would be withdrawn in September 1980 numbered 25 021. *(I.S. Carr/ARPT)*

Sunday 29 July 1963. This atmospheric photograph taken inside the cavernous interior of York station shows English Electric Type 4 (Class 40) no. D353 drifting through with a southbound parcels train. Entering service during July 1961 this locomotive would be withdrawn in September 1983 numbered 40 153. *(Eric Treacy/NRM)*

Saturday 3 August 1963. The unique diesel electric locomotive no. DP2 is seen here in its original green livery approaching York, working the 10.10 London King's Cross to Edinburgh express. Constructed by English Electric as a testbed for an improved Type 4 engine, it entered service during May 1962. The locomotive worked on the Midland, Eastern and North Eastern Regions before being involved in a collision at Thirsk on 31 July 1967. It never worked again and was scrapped in August of the same year. *(S.A. Solly)*

Saturday 24 August 1963. English Electric Type 3 (Class 37) no. D6811 is seen passing Dringhouses Marshalling Yard, just south of York, with a Scarborough to Swindon working. The three vehicles immediately behind the locomotive were attached at York. They include the Pullman Car *Eunice* and ex-LNWR Royal Mail coach no. M30209. The locomotive was constructed in February 1963 and allocated new to Sheffield Darnall depot. By 1993 it would be working out of Inverness depot before being withdrawn during September 1998. In TOPS it would be numbered 37 111 then 37 326 and finally 37 111 again. *(P.J. Lynch)*

Saturday 24 August 1963. 350hp 0–6–0 (Class 08) shunter no. D3071 shunts conflat wagons carrying 'Drikold' containers at Dringhouses. Constructed at Darlington Works in November 1953 this locomotive was originally numbered 13071 and would be withdrawn in July 1976 numbered 08 057 in TOPS. In the background, the low evening sun highlights the players in this timeless scene showing a division one game in the York and District Senior Cricket League at Dringhouses Cricket Club. *(P.J. Lynch)*

Monday 26 August 1963. Seen here parked in the yard at Hull Dairycoates depot is English Electric Type 3 (Class 37) no. D6732. Built in March 1962 it would be numbered 37 032, then 37 353 and 37 032 again before being withdrawn after thirty-two years of service in March 1994. It was purchased for preservation and is currently based at the North Norfolk Railway. *(N.E. Preedy)*

Monday 26 August 1963. This BRC&W four-unit (Class 104) DMU is seen departing from Scarborough station on a service to Hull. In the background 204hp 0–6–0 (Class 03) shunter no. D2151 is working as station pilot. Constructed at Swindon Works in July 1960 it would be numbered 03 151 in TOPS and was withdrawn during July 1985. *(P.H. Wells)*

Wednesday 28 August 1963. With the local Royal Mail van parked on the platform a Metro-Cammell two-car (Class 101) DMU waits to depart Clayton West with a service to Huddersfield and Bradford. This branch had been opened in September 1879 from Clayton West Junction principally to serve some collieries in the area. It was finally closed by British Railways in January 1983 with the track being lifted soon afterwards. The site of Clayton West station is now the base for the Kirklees Light Railway, a 15in gauge railway operating steam trains for a distance of 4 miles on the trackbed of the original branch with its current terminus at Shelley. *(Leslie Sandler)*

September 1963. Taking the fast through track at Selby station, Brush Type 2 (Class 30) no. D5570 heads a northbound express. Entering service during December 1959 this locomotive was re-engined in 1965 and would be withdrawn from service thirty years later in June 1989 numbered 31 152. *(A.A. Solly)*

Opposite top: **Monday 2 September 1963**. Preceded by a brake tender, BR/Sulzer Type 2 (Class 25) no. D5169 is seen departing westbound from Leyburn station with the daily pick-up goods. This route through Wensleydale between Northallerton and Hawes Junction and Garsdale, opened throughout in 1878 with part of the line including Leyburn station opening earlier in November 1855. The whole line was closed to passenger traffic in April 1954 with the section beyond Redmire to Garsdale closed to all traffic during April 1964 and subsequently lifted. Quarry and Ministry of Defence traffic kept the remaining line open until December 1992 when the quarry traffic ceased. Now run by the Wensleydale Railway, which was formed in 1990, the long-term aim is to re-open the whole route again. Initially the 12-mile section from Leeming Bar to Leyburn was re-opened in July 2003 followed by the 5-mile section between Leyburn and Redmire during August 2004. The locomotive in this photograph is another Darlington-constructed example of this class and was built during December 1961, being withdrawn in September 1980 numbered 25 019. *(P.H. Wells)*

Opposite bottom: **Friday 6 September 1963**. Near Leyburn again with the Down daily pick-up goods approaching the station with BR/Sulzer Type 2 (Class 25) no. D5171 in charge. *(P.H. Wells)*

Friday 6 September 1963. BR/Sulzer 'Peak' Type 4 (Class 46) no. D183 is approaching Ferryhill station at speed with an Up express. Not quite a year old having entered service during October 1962, it would be allocated to Gateshead depot and be numbered 46 046 in TOPS and was withdrawn in May 1984. *(P.H. Wells)*

Saturday 25 January 1964. At the Lady Ann Crossing signal-box near Batley, a three-car Metro-Cammell (Class 101) DMU is working a Leeds to Huddersfield service. *(John K. Morton)*

Tuesday 11 February 1964. At Morpeth station the 08.43 Newcastle to Alnwick service waits to depart. The leading car of this Metro-Cammell four-car (Class 101) set is no. E50238. *(B.J. Ashworth)*

Wednesday 12 February 1964. The immense architectural structure of the roof canopy at York station is shown here in detail as the background to this Metro-Cammell two-car (Class 101) DMU waiting to depart with the 13.09 stopping service to Leeds City station. *(B.J. Ashworth)*

Saturday 7 March 1964. English Electric Type 4 (Class 40) no. D355 is here seen taking the Sheffield route at Chaloners Whin Junction, south of York, with a class 7 goods which consists mainly of cattle wagons. Entering service during August 1961 this locomotive would be numbered 40 155 and was withdrawn in January 1985. *(J.S. Hancock)*

Sunday 5 April 1964. English Electric Deltic Type 5 (Class 55) no. D9014 *The Duke of Wellington's Regiment* tops the 1 in 78 climb out of Sunderland to Fawcett Street Junction with the 13.15 Newcastle to Sunderland and London King's Cross passenger train. This was being diverted via Cox Green and Sedgefield due to Sunday engineering works on the East Coast Main Line. First seeing service in September 1961 the locomotive was allocated to Gateshead depot and was named at a ceremony at Darlington in October 1963. It would be withdrawn from service in November 1981 numbered 55 014. *(I.S. Carr/ARPT)*

Friday 10 April 1964. Emerging from under the new station roof at Leeds City station, English Electric Type 4 (Class 40) no. D387 is working a Liverpool to Newcastle train. One of the last examples of the class to be constructed, this locomotive was introduced to service during April 1962 and it would be withdrawn just over twenty years later in August 1982 numbered 40 187. *(P.G. Moore)*

Wednesday 29 April 1964. Behind a brand new Brush Type 4 (Class 47) no. D1576, the Up 'Northumbrian', Newcastle to London King's Cross express is seen speeding south near Chaloners Whin. This service was another post-war introduction by British Railways during 1949 and although the name ceased being used in 1963, both railwaymen and enthusiasts continued its unofficial use for a similarly timed train for many years. The locomotive was one of the Crewe Works-built examples entering service earlier in the month of this photograph and allocated new to Gateshead. It would be numbered 47 456 in TOPS and was withdrawn during September 1991. *(Eric Treacy/NRM)*

Wednesday 29 April 1964. At Chaloners Whin again with Brush Type 4 (Class 47) no. D1528 hurrying a Glasgow to London King's Cross service southbound. This example of the class was one of the Loughborough-built locomotives which entered service during July 1963. Initially allocated to Finsbury Park depot, it would be withdrawn in October 1991 numbered 47 006. *(Eric Treacy/NRM)*

Wednesday 29 April 1964. English Electric Type 3 (Class 37) no. D6803 is heading a York to Lincoln train at Chaloners Whin. Entering service in January 1963 it would be numbered 37 103, then 37 511 and finally 37 607. Allocated new to Sheffield Darnall depot, by 1986 it would be based at Cardiff Canton and as at 2010 it was still in service. *(Eric Treacy/NRM)*

Wednesday 13 May 1964. Wending its way through the countryside near Marsden, south-west of Huddersfield, is BR/Sulzer 'Peak' Type 4 (Class 46) no. D182 heading a morning Liverpool to Newcastle train. The locomotive was a product of Derby Works, entering service during September 1962. It would be numbered 46 045 and withdrawn during November 1984 being taken into departmental stock numbered 97404. It would finally be withdrawn in 1992 and sold into the preservation scene currently being based at the Midland Railway Centre at Butterley. *(J.S. Whiteley)*

Wednesday 13 May 1964. The countryside near Marsden is seen again here with Swindon-built 'Trans-Pennine' six-car (Class 124) DMU working a service from Hull to Liverpool. First introduced during 1960 to operate this route, these units were powered by 240hp Leyland engines and they would operate this busy and demanding route until being withdrawn in 1984. *(J.S. Whiteley)*

Wednesday 27 May 1964. In ex-works condition having just arrived from the builders, Clayton Type 1 (Class 17) no. D8590 sits in the yard at Thornaby coupled to sister locomotive no. D8591. Primarily designed to haul goods trains, they suffered from being introduced at the wrong time as the Beeching Report had already forecast the end of wagon load traffic. They also suffered from engine problems that meant they spent a great deal of time out of traffic for maintenance and repair. In consequence they were not seen as reliable and worthy of retaining so were gradually withdrawn throughout the late 1960s with the last being withdrawn in 1971. A total of 117 were constructed with the largest allocations going into the Scottish Region. The final batch of twenty-nine locomotives including the above example, would be constructed by Beyer Peacock and were allocated to the North Eastern Region. No. D8590 would be withdrawn in March 1971 but one example of the class, D8568, survived to be sold into industrial use, eventually finding its way into the preserved scene where it is currently to be seen at the Chinnor and Princes Risborough Railway in Oxfordshire. *(J.M. Boyes/ARPT)*

Sunday 7 June 1964. English Electric Type 4 (Class 40) no. D222 *Laconia* of Longsight (9A) depot, arrives at Sunderland station with the 18.25 Newcastle to Birmingham service. The locomotive entered service during August 1959 and would be named at a ceremony in Crewe Works during October 1962. The name *Laconia* had been borne by two Cunard liners, the first being launched on 27 July 1911 only to be sunk by a German U-boat six years later on 25 November 1917. The second liner to bear the name was launched on 9 April 1921 and survived somewhat longer but its fate was also to be at the hands of a U-boat, being sunk on 12 September 1942. D222 would be numbered 40 022 in TOPS and was eventually withdrawn in March 1983. *(I.S. Carr/ARPT)*

Saturday 4 July 1964. English Electric Type 4 (Class 40) no. D248 is seen departing from Sunderland station with the 10.35 Newcastle to Filey Holiday Camp special train. Entering service during November 1959 and initially allocated to Finsbury Park depot, this locomotive would be numbered 40 048 and was withdrawn from service in October 1977. *(I.S. Carr/ARPT)*

Saturday 4 July 1964. Accelerating away from Sunderland towards the south tunnel entrance with the 10.00 Sunderland to Manchester Exchange service is BR/Sulzer 'Peak' Type 4 (Class 46) no. D181. A product of Derby Works in September 1962 it would become number 46 044 in TOPS and was withdrawn in April 1984. *(I.S. Carr/ARPT)*

Saturday 8 August 1964. Approaching Selby station is English Electric Type 4 (Class 40) no. D275 in charge of a relief Newcastle to York and Yarmouth express. A York-allocated example of the type which entered service during May 1960, this engine would become no. 40 075 in TOPS and was withdrawn in December 1981. *(Author's Collection)*

Monday 31 August 1964. On the Whitby to Pickering route, a three-car Metro-Cammell (Class 101) DMU is seen passing the disused Goathland Summit 'box while working the 11.48 Whitby to Malton and York service. Car no. E50643 is leading. *(John Clarke)*

Tuesday 1 September 1964. At Ravenscar station the signalman and the driver of the 14.15 Middlesbrough to Whitby and Scarborough service exchange tokens for the single line. The leading car of this three-car BRC&W (Class 104) DMU is no. E50598. The station was opened by the Scarborough and Whitby Railway during July 1885 and it would be closed as part of the Beeching Report cuts in March 1965. *(John Clarke)*

Thursday 3 September 1964. At Goathland station this three-car Metro-Cammell (Class 101) DMU is waiting to return to Whitby as the 13.30 service. Car no. E50196 is nearest the camera. After closure during March 1965, the station would be carefully restored as part of the North Yorkshire Moors Railway. Note the camping coach in the background. *(John Clarke)*

Saturday 3 October 1964. This wonderfully atmospheric photograph shows BR/Sulzer 'Peak' Type 4 (Class 46) no. D175 waiting to depart from York station with the 12.05 train to Newcastle. Constructed at Derby Works and entering service during August 1962 this locomotive would be withdrawn in March 1982 numbered 46 038. *(Brian Stephenson)*

Opposite top: **Saturday 3 October 1964**. This Metro-Cammell two-car (Class 101) DMU is operating the 14.32 Bradford Forster Square to Leeds City stopping service, seen here near Apperley Bridge. The leading car is no. E56055. *(Brian Stephenson)*

Opposite bottom: **Saturday 3 October 1964**. A long way from its home depot, BR/Sulzer 'Peak' Type 4 (Class 45) no. D36 bearing an 82A Bristol Bath Road shed code, waits to depart from York station with the 21.30 passenger train to Bristol. Constructed at Derby Works during July 1961 this locomotive would be withdrawn almost twenty years later in May 1981 numbered 45 031. *(Brian Stephenson)*

Saturday 3 October 1964. The interior of the magnificent station roof at York is well illuminated while English Electric Type 4 (Class 40) no. D254, bearing a 50A York shed code plate, has just arrived with a train from Scarborough. Note that the first two vehicles behind the locomotive are six-wheeled vans. Entering service in December 1959 it would be numbered 40 054 in Tops and withdrawn during December 1977. *(Brian Stephenson)*

Opposite top: **Saturday 24 October 1964.** BR/Sulzer Type 2 (Class 25) no. D5178, propelling a brake tender, is seen approaching Pelaw South Junction with a Tyne Yard to Consett empty wagon train. A product of Darlington Works during February 1963 it would be withdrawn in December 1980 numbered 25 028. *(Brian Stephenson)*

Opposite bottom: **Saturday 24 October 1964.** With the distinctive outline of the Alnwick station building in the background, a three-car Metro-Cammell (Class 101) DMU is seen departing with a service to Newcastle. The leading car is no. E50746. Note the splendid signal gantry bearing both upper and lower quadrant signals. *(C.J.B. Sanderson/ARPT)*

Saturday 24 October 1964. BR/Sulzer 'Peak' Type 4 (Class 46) no. D167 is in charge of the 10.15 Newcastle to London King's Cross passenger train seen here between Croxdale and Ferryhill. A Derby Works-built locomotive from May 1962 it would be allocated new to Gateshead depot and withdrawn in December 1980 numbered 46 030. *(Brian Stephenson)*

Opposite top: **Tuesday 2 March 1965**. With the remains of a recent snowfall still in evidence, a three-car BRC&W (Class 110) DMU has just departed from Mytholmroyd station, on the Calder Valley line, with an afternoon Leeds Central to Manchester service. *(M. York)*

Opposite bottom: **Saturday 6 March 1965**. Two days prior to the official closure of this station, the 12.50 Middlesbrough to Whitby and Scarborough service is being operated by a three-car Metro-Cammell (Class 101) DMU seen here at Robin Hood's Bay. Opened in July 1885 by the Scarborough and Whitby Railway, this closure was one of the Beeching Report cuts. The station buildings are still in situ and occupied. *(Maurice S. Burns/ARPT)*

Saturday 13 March 1965. This very unusual Charter working from Coventry brings the Warwickshire County Rugby team into West Hartlepool station using one of the Western Region Blue Pullman sets. Warwickshire were playing County Durham in the final of the Rugby Union County Championships – Warwickshire won 15–9. *(I.S. Carr/ARPT)*

Saturday 13 March 1965. The background to this photograph shows the heavy industrial scene of the Cargo Fleet Iron Works. In the foreground English Electric Type 3 (Class 37) no. D6761 propels its train of empty mineral wagons past Cargo Fleet inner signal-box into the inner yard. This locomotive was constructed in October 1962 and would be numbered 37 061, then 37 799 in TOPS and it would be allocated new to Thornaby depot. It was one of several examples of the class transferred to Spain in 2001 to work on the construction of the new standard gauge high speed line between Madrid and Barcelona. It would be returned to the UK in 2003 and was withdrawn from service during 2009. *(Ian G. Holt)*

Friday 30 April 1965. Weaverthorpe station had been closed to passenger traffic in 1930 but the signal-box there was still of importance in controlling the level crossing. This four-car BRC&W (Class 104) DMU is operating the 14.40 Leeds City to Scarborough service as it speeds through the station. *(John Clarke)*

Saturday 5 June 1965. The photographer has captured a most unusual scene of two English Electric Type 4s (Class 40) working in tandem. The 09.00 train from Liverpool Lime Street is seen entering Newcastle behind no. D256 leading no. D244, an impressive array of horse power. The former locomotive entered service during January 1960 and was withdrawn in September 1984 numbered 40 056. *(I.S. Carr/ARPT)*

Sunday 4 July 1965. At Newcastle station, BR/Sulzer Type 2 (Class 24) no. D5150, bearing a Gateshead (52A) shed code, waits to depart with a train to London King's Cross via Sunderland, while on the right an Edinburgh to London King's Cross passenger train waits to depart behind English Electric Deltic Type 5 (Class 55) no. D9013 *The Black Watch*. The Deltic entered service in September 1961 and was named during a ceremony at Dundee West station in January 1963. It would be numbered 55 013 in TOPS and was withdrawn just over twenty years later in December 1981. D5150 was a product of Derby Works during January 1961 and it would be numbered 24 150 before being withdrawn from service in December 1976. *(I.S. Carr/ARPT)*

Opposite top: **Saturday 17 July 1965.** This train is probably the late running 13.25 Manchester Victoria to Bradford and Harrogate service and it is seen here approaching the closed station at Arthington operated by two three-car BRC&W (Class 110) DMUs. *(Michael Mensing)*

Opposite bottom: **Tuesday 17 August 1965.** Speeding through the centre roads at Crossgates station near Leeds, this Swindon-built six-car (Class 124) 'Trans-Pennine' DMU is operating a Liverpool to Hull service. *(J.H. Cooper-Smith)*

Friday 4 September 1965. Denby Dale station is looking rather forlorn as a Metro-Cammell (Class 101) two-car DMU departs with the 15.07 Penistone to Huddersfield service. Note that both of these units are power cars. Today the town is served by Northern Rail services between Huddersfield, Penistone and Sheffield and the station as seen here has long since been demolished and replaced by the ubiquitous bus shelter on what is now the single track section of this route. *(Michael Mensing)*

Opposite top: **Sunday 3 October 1965**. Members of the permanent way gang watch as Brush Type 4 (Class 47) no. D1581 negotiates the realigned Up road out of Sunderland station with the 13.30 Newcastle to Sunderland and London King's Cross service. A Crewe Works-built example of the class allocated new to Gateshead during May 1964, it would, by 1968, be working out of Haymarket in Edinburgh. This locomotive was involved in an accident during November 1990 and was withdrawn from service in March 1991 numbered 47 461 in TOPS. *(I.S. Carr/ARPT)*

Opposite bottom: **Sunday 27 February 1966**. Brush-built Type 4 (Class 47) no. D1983 is seen at Reedsmarshal East Junction working a York to Edinburgh parcels train. The train was being diverted via Stockton-on-Tees, Norton West and Ferryhill to avoid Sunday engineering work on the East Coast Main Line. Another Crewe Works-constructed member of this class which entered service during December 1965, it was allocated to Gateshead and withdrawn in December 1998 numbered 47 281. *(John M. Boyes/ARPT)*

Saturday 7 May 1966. At the head of the 12.00 noon Newcastle to Lincoln and London King's Cross service, English Electric Deltic Type 5 (Class 55) no. D9018 *Ballymoss* is seen approaching Pontop Crossing as it makes its way towards Sunderland. Named at Doncaster in November 1961, the same month as it entered service, it was allocated to Finsbury Park depot and would be withdrawn in October 1981 numbered 55 018. The track in the foreground, crossing the main Newcastle to Sunderland track, was the direct route from Tyne Dock to Consett. *(I.S. Carr/ARPT)*

Opposite top: **Thursday 24 March 1966**. The gently rolling nature of the hills in this North Yorkshire scene are evident as two two-car Metro-Cammell (Class 101) DMUs operate the 16.08 Whitby Town to Middlesbrough service near Kildale station on the Grosmont to Battersby section of this line. *(John M. Boyes/ARPT)*

Opposite bottom: **Thursday 14 April 1966**. Seen arriving at Durham Gilesgate goods station is Clayton Type 1 (Class 17) no. D8596 with the daily goods train from the Tyne Yard. The locomotive was one of the examples constructed by Beyer Peacock entering service in July 1964 to be withdrawn only four years later during December 1968. Gilesgate station in Durham was the original terminus of the Newcastle and Durham Junction Railway which opened in 1844. It was replaced by the present station in 1857 and survived as a goods depot until closure in 1966. The building is now occupied by a hotel. *(I.S. Carr/ARPT)*

Saturday 21 May 1966. The photographer has braved the pouring rain to capture this shot of BR/Sulzer 'Peak' Type 4 (Class 45) no. D68 crossing the High Level Bridge over the River Tyne and approaching Newcastle Central station with a train from Liverpool. This example of the class was constructed at Crewe Works, entering service during October 1960. It would be withdrawn in August 1988 numbered 45 046 in TOPS. *(A.R. Thompson/ARPT)*

Saturday 21 May 1966. On the same day as the previous photograph, this time in bright sunshine, English Electric Type 3 (Class 37) no. D6773, together with a brake tender, is seen near Beningbrough on the East Coast Main Line with an Up goods train. Coming into service during September 1962, this example of the class was built at the Robert Stephenson and Hawthorn Works of English Electric and would eventually be numbered 37 073. Having been originally allocated to Thornaby depot, by 1994 it would be based at Motherwell. This was another well-travelled locomotive making its way in July 1999 to the south of France to assist in the construction of a new TGV high speed line. It returned to the UK during October 2000 and was finally withdrawn in April 2003. *(C.W.R. Bowman)*

Saturday 28 May 1966. English Electric Deltic Type 5 (Class 55) no. D9014 *The Duke of Wellington's Regiment* is seen here crossing Plawsworth Viaduct near Durham while hauling a London King's Cross to Glasgow service. *(A.R. Thompson/ARPT)*

Saturday 18 June 1966. English Electric Type 4 (Class 40) no. D283 is seen passing Standon Crossing near West Hartlepool while in charge of a Newcastle to Colchester service. Initially allocated to York depot this locomotive was brought into service during July 1960 and would be withdrawn in November 1981 numbered 40 083. *(J.S. Hancock)*

Wednesday 22 June 1966. This atmospheric shot shows Brush Type 4 (Class 47) no. D1895 approaching the hopper house at Ferrybridge 'C' Power Station with a train of automatic discharge hopper wagons carrying coal. One of the Brush, Loughborough-constructed members of the class, it entered service during September 1965 and was allocated to Sheffield Darnall, though by the time of this photograph it was based at Leeds Holbeck depot. It would be withdrawn in June 2001 numbered 47 376. This example would be sold into the preservation scene and is currently based at the Gloucester and Warwickshire Railway at Toddington. *(Author's Collection)*

Thursday 7 July 1966. Prior to the withdrawal of the BR Standard Class 9F 2–10–0 steam locomotives on the Tyne Dock to Consett iron ore traffic, trials were carried out with BR/Sulzer Type 2s. Two of these locomotives were specially equipped to operate these trains, nos D5112 and D5180. Here we see the latter locomotive approaching Beamish with a train bound for Consett together with heavy weight banking power in the form of English Electric Type 4 (Class 40) no. D257 pushing in the rear. D5180 was one of the Darlington-constructed examples of the class which entered service in February 1963 but which became one of the early withdrawals of the class in August 1976 numbered 25 030. *(G. McLean)*

Tuesday 16 August 1966. Another Darlington Works-built locomotive, BR/Sulzer Type 2 (Class 25) no. D5181 is passing Hedworth Lane 'box with a Tyne Dock to Consett iron ore train. Entering service in March 1963 it would be withdrawn during December 1977 numbered 25 031. *(I.S. Carr/ARPT)*

Thursday 25 August 1966. This Robert Stephenson and Hawthorn Works-constructed, English Electric Type 3 (Class 37) no. D6777 is approaching Newcastle having come off the line from Carlisle with a train of oil tanks. Coming ex-works in October 1962 it was allocated to Thornaby depot and by 1988 it was working out of Stratford depot. Another of the class to work in France, it left the UK in September 1999 and returned during July 2000. It would be numbered 37 077 in TOPS and was withdrawn in June 2009. *(John H. Bird/Southern-images.co.uk)*

Friday 26 August 1966. This three-car Metro-Cammell (Class 101) DMU is seen arriving at West Hartlepool with a service for Newcastle. *(John H. Bird/Southern-images.co.uk)*

Tuesday 27 September 1966. Seen just north of West Hartlepool, BR/Sulzer Type 2 (Class 24) no. D5097 is working a northbound parcels train. Constructed at Darlington Works and introduced to service in May 1960 it would be withdrawn during February 1976 numbered 24 097. *(Michael Mensing)*

Tuesday 27 September 1966. During the afternoon of this misty day, BR/Sulzer Type 2 (Class 24) no. D5106 is seen drawing out of Stockton-on-Tees yard with a train of full coal hopper wagons. A product of Darlington Works during September 1960, this locomotive would survive for only sixteen years before being withdrawn during December 1976 numbered 24 106 in TOPS. *(Michael Mensing)*

Wednesday 28 September 1966. South of Durham, Crewe Works-constructed Brush Type 4 (Class 47) no. D1580 is in charge of a long train of empty mineral wagons. The crew of this locomotive are showing a headlamp code in addition to the four-character train code. Entering service and allocated to Gateshead depot in May 1964, by 1968 it would be based at Haymarket in Edinburgh and it was withdrawn during January 1992 numbered 47 460. *(Michael Mensing)*

Wednesday 28 September 1966. At the same location as the previous photograph, BR/Sulzer 'Peak' Type 4 (Class 46) no. D174 is also showing a headlamp code in addition to the four-character train code. A Derby Works-built example of the class, this locomotive was introduced to service during July 1962 and it would be withdrawn in June 1984 numbered 46 037. *(Michael Mensing)*

Opposite top: **Saturday 10 December 1966**. Parked in the yard at Wakefield depot (56A) is English Electric Type 3 (Class 37) no. D6736. *(K.P. Lawrence)*

Opposite bottom: **Saturday 28 January 1967**. This grimy looking BR/Sulzer Type 2 (Class 25) no. D5158 is heading a local trip working from Grangetown to Tees Yard Middlesbrough and is seen near Cargo Fleet on the Middlesbrough to Saltburn line. Note the shunter's pole in the usual handy position on the bufferbeam. Constructed at Darlington Works in July 1961 the locomotive would become numbered 25 008 and was withdrawn from service in June 1980. *(John M. Boyes/ARPT)*

Tuesday 14 February 1967. Waskerley goods station was situated high up on the moors beyond Tow Law and although opening as early as 1845, it only sustained a passenger service until 1859. Constructed to tap the rich limestone deposits in the Weardale area, the goods service survived until the late 1960s. Here we see 350hp 0–6–0 (Class 08) shunter no. D3875 propelling wagons onto the weighbridge. A product of Crewe Works during March 1960 it would serve until withdrawn in October 1992 numbered 08 708. The old trackbed is now part of the Waskerley Way footpath. *(G. Robson)*

Opposite top: **Saturday 11 March 1967**. This splendid photograph shows another Crewe Works-constructed example of the class, Brush Type 4 (Class 47) no. D1582 heading south from Durham with a fitted goods train. Coming into service during May 1964 and allocated to Gateshead it would be numbered 47 462 in TOPS and was withdrawn from service during 2002. *(G. Gwilliam)*

Opposite bottom: **Saturday 11 March 1967**. Brush Type 4 (Class 47) no. D1103 is seen here just south of Durham heading a Down train for Newcastle. Entering service during October 1966, this Crewe Works-built example would be numbered 47 520 and was withdrawn in August 1998. This example of the class would also be allocated to York and by the time of this photograph was based at Gateshead depot. *(G. Gwilliam)*

Saturday 20 May 1967. Bearing a 41C (Millhouses shed allocation) under its number, English Electric Type 3 (Class 37) no. D6959 awaits its next duty at Hull Dairycoates depot. Entering service during January 1965 it would initially be allocated to Sheffield Darnall depot and by 1987 it was working out of Cardiff Canton. In TOPS it would be numbered 37 259, then 37 380 and finally 37 259 again. It is currently owned by Direct Rail Services and is still used in main line service. *(David Percival)*

Opposite top: **Friday 29 March 1967**. Clayton Type 1 (Class 17) no. D8594 is seen here trundling through Wallsend station with a local pick-up goods. Constructed by Beyer Peacock during June 1964 this locomotive would be withdrawn in September 1971. *(I.S. Carr/ARPT)*

Opposite bottom: **Friday 28 April 1967**. English Electric Type 4 (Class 40) no. D352 is seen here with an Up goods train between Norton West and Norton South signal-boxes. *(J.M. Boyes/ARPT)*

Monday 12 June 1967. BR/Sulzer 'Peak' Type 4 (Class 46) no. D166 hurries a Newcastle to York via Bishop Auckland parcels train near Brancepeth. A product of Derby Works which entered service during May 1962 and allocated to Gateshead, it would be numbered 46 029 in TOPS and was withdrawn in January 1983. *(Ian R. Smith)*

Opposite top: **Saturday 20 May 1967**. With Class K1 2–6–0 no. 62005 at the head of the train, the SLS 'Three Dales Railtour' has reached Redmire, the terminus station on the remainder of the Hawes branch through Wensleydale. Meanwhile, at the rear of the train, the crew of BR/Sulzer Type 2 (Class 25) no. D5160, sporting a 51L (Thornaby) shed code, wait patiently for the restart. The diesel locomotive had been added to the train specifically for this branch as the run-round loop at Redmire could not accommodate a six-coach train. A product of Darlington Works in August 1961 this locomotive would be withdrawn during December 1980 numbered 25 010. *(John M. Boyes/ARPT)*

Opposite bottom: **Thursday 8 June 1967**. BR/Sulzer 'Peak' Type 4 (Class 46) no. D182 is seen here negotiating the characteristically North Eastern Railway signal-box construction at Church Street, west Hartlepool. The train is the 11.05 Newcastle to York parcels which includes in the rake a Gresley-designed buffet car. *(John M. Boyes/ARPT)*

Saturday 17 June 1967. Brush Type 4 (Class 47) no. D1800 accelerates through Hebden Bridge station with a Blackpool to Lincoln passenger train. Constructed at the Loughborough Works of Brush during January 1965 and allocated new to Sheffield Darnall, this locomotive would be withdrawn during 1998 numbered 47 319. *(J.H. Cooper-Smith)*

Opposite top: **Monday 19 June 1967**. Five weeks before it suffered terminal damage in an accident at Thirsk on 31 July of this year, we see the experimental locomotive no. DP2 at York station bearing its later more striking multi-green livery. *(Peter J. Robinson/ARPT)*

Opposite bottom: **Saturday 8 July 1967**. With the city of Leeds spread out in the background, English Electric Type 4 (Class 40) no. D246 climbs towards Morley with the 09.14 (SO) Leeds City to Llandudno train. This locomotive entered service during November 1959 and was allocated new to Gateshead. It would be withdrawn in February 1983 numbered 40 046. *(M. Mitchell)*

Thursday 24 August 1967. With the imminent closure of the last two steam locomotive depots in the area at Sunderland and West Hartlepool, trials were undertaken with diesel traction on the Silksworth Colliery branch. Seen here are a pair of 204hp 0–6–0 (Class 03) shunters, no. D2074 leading no. D2071, approaching Ryhope while working a heavy train of coal hopper wagons. Both locomotives were constructed at Doncaster Works during October and November 1959 with both being withdrawn from service in May 1972. In the background is the massive bulk of St Paul's Church in Ryhope. *(E. Knight)*

Opposite top: **Saturday 29 July 1967.** Sitting under the roof canopy at Bradford Exchange station, English Electric Type 4 (Class 40) no. D356 waits to depart with the 17.20 service to Leeds City. *(R.F. Roberts/SLS)*

Opposite bottom: **Friday 18 August 1967.** Photographed during a thunderstorm, Clayton-built Type 1 (Class 17) no. D8592 is seen passing Cox Green station with the afternoon Pallion to Tyne Yard goods train. Constructed by Beyer Peacock and introduced to service during May 1964, this locomotive had a short working life of just over seven years before being withdrawn in September 1971. *(I.S. Carr/ARPT)*

Thursday 7 September 1967. Clayton Type 1 (Class 17) no. D8595 is seen leaving the sidings at Ryhope Grange after running round the goods train which it had brought down the branch from Sunderland Dock. Another example of the Beyer Peacock-constructed members of this class, it entered service during June 1964 and had one of the shortest working lives of only four and a half years, being withdrawn from service in December 1968. *(J.S. Hancock)*

Sunday 10 September 1967. This excellent photograph shows English Electric Type 5 Deltic no. D9017 *The Durham Light Infantry* crossing Plawsworth Viaduct at the head of the 16.00 Edinburgh to London King's Cross express. *(J.M. Boyes/ARPT)*

Thursday 19 October 1967. The Royal Train was being used on this day to facilitate the queen's visit to the north-east of England to officially open the Tyne Tunnel. Seen here at Norton-on-Tees east curve is a Crewe Works-built example of the class, Brush Type 4 (Class 47) no. D1985 with the Royal Train heading from Billingham to Darlington. Entering service in January 1966 and based at Gateshead, the locomotive would be withdrawn during 2003 numbered 47 283. *(John M. Boyes/ARPT)*

Saturday 28 October 1967. This wonderfully atmospheric photograph shows English Electric Type 4 (Class 40) no. D285 sitting in a pool of light inside Huddersfield station. It is working the 09.50 service from Newcastle to Liverpool Lime Street. This locomotive entered service during July 1960 and was allocated to York depot. It would be withdrawn in March 1984 numbered 40 085. *(John H. Bird/Southern-images.co.uk)*

Thursday 28 December 1967. English Electric Type 3 (Class 37) no. D6757 waits for the 'right of way' at Cargo Fleet station at the head of a Grangetown to Tees Yard goods train. Entering service during October 1962 this locomotive would be allocated new to Thornaby depot but by 1981 it was working from Stratford depot. Numbered 37 057 in TOPS, it is currently owned by Harry Needle Rail and is being held in store at the Barrow Hill Roundhouse. *(John M. Boyes/ARPT)*

Opposite top: **Saturday 6 January 1968**. Having arrived at platform 9 in York station, Brush Type 4 (Class 47) no. D1607 waits to depart with the 08.15 Cardiff to Newcastle service. Constructed at Crewe Works and allocated new to Landore depot in Wales, it entering service during July 1964 and would be withdrawn in November 1992 numbered 47 477. *(David Wharton)*

Opposite bottom: **Saturday 9 March 1968**. This Metro-Cammell (Class 101) DMU is working the 13.40 Newcastle to Hexham service seen here passing the cottage at North Wylam where George Stephenson was born in 1781. This line joined the Newcastle to Carlisle route at West Wylam Junction and it would be closed during 1968. *(I.S. Carr/ARPT)*

Saturday 9 March 1968. The destination blind may show Newsham but this Metro-Cammell (Class 101) DMU is working the 13.07 Hexham to Newcastle service seen here crossing the River Tyne near West Wylam Junction. This beautifully arched structure, known as Points Bridge, was constructed in wrought iron and opened in 1876. The line on the north bank of the River Tyne closed during 1968 and the bridge is now part of a National Footpath. *(I.S. Carr/ARPT)*

Saturday 30 March 1968. With huge spoil heaps in the background, two two-car Metro-Cammell (Class 101) DMUs are approaching West Wylam Junction, near Prudhoe, with the 14.20 Carlisle to Newcastle service. *(John M. Boyes/ARPT)*

Saturday 27 April 1968. English Electric Type 3 (Class 37) no. D6760 has arrived at Redmire with the 08.30 empty limestone hoppers from the Tees Yard and has run round its train before propelling the wagons into the quarry reception yard. Entering service during October 1962 the locomotive would be allocated firstly to Thornaby depot but by 1981 it would be based at Stratford. In TOPS it would be numbered 37 060, then 37 705 and it was withdrawn from service in July 2007 having given forty-five years' service. *(J.M. Boyes/ARPT)*

Saturday 4 May 1968. Brush Type 4 (Class 47) no. D1873 is seen passing Pegswood Colliery with a Down express. The locomotive was a product of the Brush Works at Loughborough entering service during May 1965 and allocated new to Sheffield Darnall. It would be withdrawn thirty-five years' later during May 2000 numbered 47 223. The colliery would be closed during 1969. *(J.M. Boyes/ARPT)*

Thursday 27 June 1968. The Alston branch service on this day was being operated by a two-car DMU consisting of one GRC&W (Class 100) power car, no. E51125, coupled to a Metro-Cammell (Class 101) car. With this formation we see here the 15.34 Haltwhistle to Alston service crossing Lambley Viaduct on the approach to Lambley station. *(Michael Mensing)*

Opposite top: **Thursday 9 May 1968**. Riding Mill station on the Newcastle to Carlisle route was opened in 1835 and is still in use today by Northern Rail services. On this day a GRC&W (Class 100) two-car DMU is working a Hexham to Newcastle local. *(J.M. Boyes/ARPT)*

Opposite bottom: **Thursday 27 June 1968**. This two-car Metro-Cammell (Class 101) DMU is seen departing Haltwhistle station with the 12.30 Newcastle to Carlisle service. In the background is the Haltwhistle Viaduct carrying the Alston branch over the River South Tyne. *(Michael Mensing)*

Sunday 2 February 1969. An unusual double heading is seen here accelerating away from Sunderland. BR/Sulzer 'Peak' Type 4 (Class 45) no. D39 is leading Brush Type 4 (Class 47) no. D1866 while working the Sunday only 13.30 Newcastle to London King's Cross service. The Derby Works-built 'Peak' entered service in July 1961 and would be withdrawn during February 1988 numbered 45 033, while the Class 47 entered service during May 1965 and would be numbered 47 216, then 47 299 in TOPS and withdrawn in April 1999. *(I.S. Carr/ARPT)*

Opposite top: **Friday 28 June 1968**. Seen passing through Wetheral station on the Carlisle to Newcastle route, is English Electric Type 3 (Class 37) no. D6833 at the head of a westbound goods train. This locomotive entered service in April 1963 and would be allocated new to Cardiff Canton depot but by 1992 it would be working out of Inverness. This was another member of the class to work in France between June 1999 and September 2000. It would finally be withdrawn during September 2003 numbered 37 133. *(Michael Mensing)*

Opposite bottom: **Tuesday 15 October 1968**. At Shilbottle Colliery sidings NCB 0–6–0ST no. 46 waits while English Electric Type 3 (Class 37) no. D6795 leaves the exchange sidings with a loaded coal train for Morpeth. The 'Austerity' had been constructed by Hunslet during 1943 and was fitted with a Giesl Ejector in 1968 only to be withdrawn in 1969. The colliery had been owned by the Co-operative Wholesale Society until its nationalisation in 1947. Departures of coal by rail ceased during 1978 and it would remain open for a few years more, closing in 1982. *(J.M. Boyes/ARPT)*

Thursday 6 February 1969. The 16.08 Whitby to Middlesbrough service, comprising a five-unit DMU made up of one three-car and one two-car Metro-Cammell (Class 101) units, has paused in Sleights station. The station is still used by Northern Rail trains operating services to Whitby although the line has since been singled, but the station buildings in this photograph are still in use. *(J.M. Boyes/ARPT)*

Opposite top: **Monday 7 April 1969**. This misty Easter Monday afternoon sees Brush Type 4 (Class 47) no. D1539 leaving Heaton Carriage Sidings with the empty coaching stock to form the 15.00 Newcastle to London King's Cross service. A product of the Brush Loughborough Works in September 1963 it would be allocated new to Sheffield Darnall and withdrawn during December 1989 numbered 47 012. *(I.S. Carr/ARPT)*

Opposite bottom: **Saturday 26 April 1969**. BR/Sulzer Type 2 (Class 25) no. D7593 runs round the coaching stock after arriving at the Tyne Commission Quay with the 14.33 boat train from Newcastle Central station. A Darlington Works-constructed example of the class, it would be numbered 25 243 in TOPS and withdrawn during September 1983. *(I.S. Carr/ARPT)*

Sunday 6 July 1969. This departure from York station on this summer Sunday is the 13.30 Newcastle to London King's Cross service behind Brush Type 4 (Class 47) no. D1764. Entering service during September 1964 and allocated new to Sheffield Darnall, this locomotive would be numbered 47 169, then 47 581 and finally 47 763 before being withdrawn in November 2000. *(David Wharton)*

Opposite top: **Sunday 6 July 1969**. Waiting to depart from York station is Brush Type 4 (Class 47) no. D1773 at the head of the 09.30 Aberdeen to London King's Cross service. Entering service during September 1964 and allocated to Sheffield Darnall, this example of the class would be numbered 47 178, then 47 588 and finally 47 737 before being withdrawn almost forty years later in February 2004. *(David Wharton)*

Opposite bottom: **Sunday 6 July 1969**. Brush Type 4 (Class 47) no. D1996 waits to leave York station with the 11.35 London King's Cross to Edinburgh service. This Crewe Works-built example entered service in June 1966 and would be withdrawn over thirty years later during September 1999 numbered 47 294. The locomotive was allocated new to York depot but by the time of this photograph was based at Gateshead depot. *(David Wharton)*

Sunday 6 July 1969. Brush Type 4 (Class 47) no. D1523 pauses in the centre roads at York station to allow a crew change to take place while working the 18.10 Scarborough to Barnsley private charter train. Coming into service during June 1963 and allocated to Finsbury Park depot, it would be numbered 47 003 in TOPS and withdrawn in March 1991. *(David Wharton)*

Opposite top: **Saturday 19 July 1969**. This fascinating photograph shows English Electric Deltic Type 5 (Class 55) no. D9000 *Royal Scots Grey*, by now painted in blue corporate livery, speeding south with the 10.10 Edinburgh to London King's Cross express as it reaches the water troughs at Wiske Moor. Entering service in February 1961 and allocated to Haymarket depot in Edinburgh, it was named during a ceremony at Edinburgh Waverley station in June 1962. Numbered 55 022 in TOPS it would be withdrawn in January 1982 and purchased for preservation. The locomotive is currently based at the East Lancashire Railway. *(I.S. Carr/ARPT)*

Opposite bottom: **Saturday 19 July 1969**. Another photograph taken at Wiske Moor troughs from the same photographer shows BR/Sulzer 'Peak' Type 4 (Class 45) no. D127 at the head of the 11.00 Inter-Regional Liverpool to Newcastle express. Constructed at Crewe Works in November 1961, this locomotive would be withdrawn in April 1985 numbered 45 072. *(I.S. Carr/ARPT)*

Friday 8 August 1969. This beautiful rural scene is at Kildale station on the line between Battersby and Grosmont, the Esk Valley route, with English Electric Type 3 (Class 37) no. D6821, coupled to a brake tender, shunting the station yard while in charge of the 05.05 Tees Yard to Whitby pick-up goods. This service was a Monday, Wednesday and Friday only working. The locomotive was a product of the English Electric Robert Stephenson and Hawthorn Works and entered service in April 1963. Initially allocated to Cardiff Canton depot, by 1966 it would be working out of Haymarket depot in Edinburgh and by the time this photograph was taken it would be based at Thornaby depot. Originally numbered 37 121 in TOPS it would be renumbered 37 677 and be withdrawn during February 2008. The scene is overlooked by the well-proportioned lines of St Cuthbert's Church, which since 1992 has contained a stained-glass window portraying a steam locomotive at Kildale station. *(John M. Boyes/ARPT)*

Opposite top: **Monday 11 August 1969**. Almost ten years after entering service this pair of grimy looking English Electric Type 1s (Class 20) are working nose to nose, a formation that later became common for the class. This train of empty hopper wagons is being hauled by no. D8023 leading sister no. D8024 through Pegswood station. Both locomotives were the product of the Robert Stephenson and Hawthorn Works in November 1959, the former being numbered 20 023 then 20 301 in TOPS and being withdrawn during May 1991. The latter was withdrawn during May 1977 numbered 20 024. *(I.S. Carr/ARPT)*

Opposite bottom: **Autumn 1969**. This pair of two-car Metro-Cammell (Class 101) DMUs, with a four-wheeled van attached to the rear, are operating the 12.35 Carlisle to Newcastle service and are seen passing the site of the disused Farnley Scar tunnel near Corbridge. Built originally as a single-track tunnel and opened in 1834, by 1844 work was being undertaken to widen the tunnel to facilitate double track. British Railways finally abandoned the tunnel in 1962 after building a deviation cutting to the south. *(K. Groundwater)*

Saturday 20 September 1969. A mystery excursion train from Manchester Piccadilly has arrived at Scarborough and this atmospheric photograph shows Brush-built Type 4 (Class 47) no. D1964 resting at the buffer stops on platform 1 while passengers alight. A product of Crewe Works during September 1965 and allocated new to Newport Ebbw Junction, it would be numbered 47 264, then 47 619 and finally 47 829. It is currently owned by Harry Needle Rail and is to be found in store at Long Marston. *(David Birch)*

Opposite top: **Thursday 30 October 1969**. Constructed at the Brush works in Loughborough in 1967 and brought into service on British Railways in January 1968, the HS4000 locomotive named *Kestrel* was the testbed for a powerful 4,000hp diesel engine. It was tested successfully over Shap with a twenty-coach train and was subsequently allocated to Tinsley depot (41A) to handle heavy coal trains. October 1969 saw it working London King's Cross to Newcastle passenger trains and here we see it at Newcastle Central station about to depart with empty coaching stock to Heaton carriage sidings. The locomotive would work the 07.55 ex-London King's Cross and return with the 16.45 service to King's Cross. By July 1971 it had been sold to the Russian Railways and was shipped to the USSR during that month. *(I.S. Carr/ARPT)*

Opposite bottom: **Saturday 2 May 1970**. This is the last day of passenger services to the Tyne Commission Quay and the 14.10 service from Newcastle Central station has been operated by a seven-car set formed by two two-car and one three-car Metro-Cammell (Class 101) DMUs. Opened as the Albert Edward Dock in 1900 to provide berths for steamers connecting to the Scandinavian countries, it was renamed the Tyne Commission Quay in 1920. *(I.S. Carr)*

Monday 1 June 1970. Awaiting its next duty at Sunderland depot is English Electric Type 3 (Class 37) no. D6765. Entering service during November 1962 and allocated to Thornaby depot it would be withdrawn over forty-five years later in December 2007 numbered 37 065. *(N.E. Preedy)*

Opposite top and bottom: **Saturday 27 June 1970**. Parked together at Sunderland diesel depot are two 350hp diesel electric 0–6–0 (Class 08) shunters. Opposite above: no. D3316 bearing the British Rail corporate logo on the cabside; formerly no. 13316 it would be numbered 08 246 in TOPS and was withdrawn during August 1982. Opposite below: no D3322 is still wearing the British Railways lion and wheel emblem. Formerly no. 13322 it would become number 08 252 in TOPS and was withdrawn in August 1981. Both locomotives had been constructed at Darlington Works, the former in September 1956 and the latter in November 1956. *(Both David Percival)*

Sunday 23 May 1971. Parked between duties at Goole is 204hp diesel mechanical 0–6–0 (Class 03) shunter no. D2159 bearing the British Rail corporate logo. It was built at Swindon Works and entered service in September 1960 and would be numbered 03 159 before being withdrawn during October 1977. *(David Wharton)*

Opposite top: **Saturday 29 August 1970**. Taking the centre road through York station, English Electric Type 3 (Class 37) no. D6778 is working the 12.50 Tees Yard to New England goods train. This locomotive is an example of the class constructed at the Robert Stephenson and Hawthorn Works. Entering service during October 1962, it would be allocated new to Thornaby depot and by 1993 it would be working out of Inverness. It would be numbered 37 078 in TOPS and give almost forty-two years' service before being withdrawn in February 2004. *(David Wharton)*

Opposite bottom: **Friday 25 September 1970**. In heavy rain, BR/Sulzer Type 2 (Class 25) no. D7545 has just departed from Durham station with a northbound parcels train. One of the Derby Works-built locomotives coming into service in May 1965, it would be numbered 25 195 in TOPS and was withdrawn during June 1985. *(I.S. Carr/ARPT)*

Thursday 29 July 1971. 350hp 0–6–0 (Class 08) shunter no. D3532 is seen at Doncaster station working as station pilot. This was a Derby Works-built example of July 1958 and would be numbered 08 417. Over fifty years later this locomotive is currently owned by Serco and based at Derby. *(Terry Whitham)*

Opposite top: **Sunday 20 June 1971**. Seen in Thornaby depot yard on this day is 204hp diesel mechanical 0–6–0 (Class 03) shunter no. D2107. A product of Doncaster Works in October 1960, it would be withdrawn in August 1981 numbered 03 107. *(David Wharton)*

Opposite bottom: **Sunday 20 June 1971**. At Thornaby depot again we see no. D2067, another Doncaster example of the 204hp 0–6–0 (Class 03) diesel mechanical. Constructed in September 1959 it would be numbered 03 067 and was also withdrawn in August 1981. *(David Wharton)*

Saturday 4 September 1971. The Alston branch, from its junction at Haltwhistle, had been saved from closure in the early 1960s owing to its vital link for the local population and the DMU-operated service was introduced on the branch on Monday 2 November 1959. The rudimentary station facilities are seen here at Coanwood with the two-car Metro-Cammell (Class 101) DMU about to depart. *(Andrew Muckley)*

Opposite top: **September 1971**. This two-car Metro-Cammell (Class 101) DMU is about to depart from Great Ayton station with a service from Whitby to Middlesbrough. This station building, on the Esk Valley route, has since been demolished and replaced by a modern structure. *(Andrew Muckley)*

Opposite bottom: **September 1971**. A two-car Metro-Cammell (Class 101) DMU is seen here departing from Lealholm station with a service from Middlesbrough to Whitby Town. The beautifully constructed stone station building is still in situ and is now used as a private house. *(Andrew Muckley)*

Saturday 4 September 1971. At Slaggyford station, a more substantial affair with a station building on the platform. The two-car Metro-Cammell (Class 101) DMU is about to depart for Haltwhistle. *(Andrew Muckley)*

Opposite top and bottom: **Saturday 4 September 1971**. At Alston station where by this time the overall roof had been removed, all the structures associated with the railway, except the station building, have also been swept away. The branch was finally closed completely in May 1976 and by 1977 a decision had been made to construct a 2ft narrow gauge line on the original trackbed. The first section of the South Tyneside Railway from Alston to Gilderdale was opened in July 1983 with the second section to Kirkhaugh being opened in September 1999. Further work is taking place to extend the line to Slaggyford where the original station building still stands. *(Both Andrew Muckley)*

Tuesday 21 September 1971. 350hp 0–6–0 (Class 08) shunter no. D3913 is seen here working as station pilot at Doncaster station. This example was a Crewe Works-built locomotive from November 1960 that would be numbered 08 745 and is currently owned by Freightliner Ltd and to be found in store at Southampton. *(Terry Whitham)*

Opposite top: **Saturday 9 September 1972**. The long Wearhead branch lost its passenger services in June 1953 and the track north of Eastgate to Wearhead was lifted. However, with the construction of a large cement works at Eastgate during 1964, goods services continued to here until 1993 when the cement works was closed and the line from Bishop Auckland was mothballed. Soon afterwards the fledgling Weardale Railway Preservation Project commenced work to bring the single line up to passenger operating standard and although suffering a chequered history the branch was reopened from Bishop Auckland to Stanhope in May 2010. In this photograph we see the rear end of the RCTS 'Northern Dales Railtour' special passing through a forlorn looking Stanhope station on its way to Eastgate. The DMU at the rear of the train is a two-car Metro-Cammell (Class 101) unit as originally built with four marker lights and destination blind. By this date it had acquired the British Rail corporate logo and a full yellow painted cab. *(Andrew Muckley)*

Opposite bottom: **April 1973**. A two-car Metro-Cammell (Class 101) DMU waits to depart from the Crook branch platform at Bishop Auckland station with a service to Darlington. Nothing remains of the buildings in this photograph, the whole being swept away during a redevelopment of the station site in the 1980s which left a single platform and a small modern station building in its place. *(Andrew Muckley)*

Monday 23 April 1973. Easter Monday sees the Alston branch service being operated by the usual two-car Metro-Cammell (Class 101) DMU. It is seen here crossing the well proportioned stone viaduct over the River South Tyne just north of Alston station. *(Andrew Muckley)*

May 1974. Even as late as this date, some diesel locomotives had still not acquired their new TOPS numbers. Seen working as Castleford yard pilot is 350hp 0–6–0 (Class 08) shunter no. D3381. Note the use, still, of the small prefix letter and the shunter's pole in the usual handy position. Constructed at Derby Works in September 1957 it would eventually become numbered 08 311 and was withdrawn during December 1982. *(J.G. Glover)*